Out of This World Ideas

And the Inventions They Inspired

Edward M. Wysocki, Jr.

To the people who are able to put up with me when I am in author mode

CONTENTS

LIST OF FIGURES

INTRODUCTION

I suppose I should begin by explaining how this book came to be written.

It all began with a book that I acquired in 1983. This book was *The Science Fiction Novel: Imagination and Social Criticism*. It is a collection of four essays, each based on a talk delivered by a science fiction author at the University of Chicago in early 1957. The talks were delivered by Robert Heinlein, C. M. Kornbluth, Alfred Bester and Robert Bloch.

As Heinlein has always been my favorite science fiction author, the essay that was of the greatest interest to me was his "Science Fiction: Its Nature, Faults and Virtues." In fact, the presence of his essay was the reason that I purchased the book. Heinlein attempted to characterize what he liked to call "speculative fiction" in a number of ways. At one point he considered the question of whether the speculations of science fiction are prophecy. His response was a definite No. For two of his stories, he explained where he had obtained the information that served as the basis for his apparently prophetic descriptions.

To further explore a connection between science fiction and science, Heinlein then presented a brief list of science fiction authors of that time who had a scientific or engineering background. He followed that with the statement that "science fiction not infrequently guides the direction of science." To back up this assertion, he related an incident from his life that affected my life for many years. He made the claim that a device used in one of his early stories served as the inspiration for one of his classmates from the Naval Academy to develop a system that was used by the Navy during World War II. If you are interested, the quote from what I have called the Virtues essay is in the Notes section.

At the time that I read that quote, Robert Heinlein was still alive. My one regret is that I never attempted during the remaining years of his life to contact him and ask him what the device was. Would he have answered me? I don't know. When other people had asked him, they were told that the device was secret. If it was really a secret, then why did Heinlein mention it in the first place?

A few years after his death, I began my search to find the answer. If you look at the quote in the Notes, you will see that Heinlein does not identify the classmate, the story, the story device or the naval system. If he had provided some information on just one of those four details, it would have made my search much easier.

The story of my search and my solution to the problem are contained in my first book *The Great Heinlein Mystery*. In the type of story that one might find in a pulp mystery magazine, one means of providing a solution is the discovery of a scrap of paper in the handwriting of the victim or possibly the guilty party. Although I did quite a bit of research over a number of years, I was never able to find the equivalent of such a scrap in a statement by Heinlein. I was finally able to arrive at an answer. Can I prove that it is the correct answer? No, but it's my answer and I am sticking with it. If you want to know what I said and why I said it, you will just have to read my first book.

For all of its complications, the basic problem was to establish a connection between an idea presented in a science fiction story and the development of an invention in the real world. Even as I was searching for the answer to the Mystery (as I called it), I asked myself how unusual a situation it was. At that time, I had never heard of a work of science fiction inspiring an invention. Was I attempting to solve the only such case that ever existed? Or were there other pairings of science fiction stories and inventions? If there were other cases, were they rare or commonplace?

I was gradually able to find a small number of cases that were worth looking at. These were very briefly described in one of the chapters of my first book. The information that I found was enough to tell me that my attempt to solve the Mystery was not an impossibility, just something that might tend to be very difficult. As it was.

When I looked back at my first book some time later, I decided that some of the cases should be examined in more detail. During online searches for more information on the topic of inventions and science fiction, I began to encounter websites that claimed that the bunch of inventions that they listed were inspired by science fiction. When I looked at many of those claims, I found that they just did not hold together. I decided to put together a serious examination of the question of science fiction and inventions.

So that is what I have done here. The greater part of the material in this book is concerned with the history behind certain inventors and their inventions and whether or not there exists a connection with a work of science fiction.

When you read the chapters, some of you may wonder why I have provided the amount of detail that I did. We cannot look into the mind of the person to see how the story idea triggered the development of the invention. What was it about the person that made him susceptible to the suggestion supplied by the story? The best I can do is to provide the details of that person's life and education and the circumstances under which the science fiction story was encountered. If you feel that I have gone on too long in some chapters, I can only say that I feel that it is always better to have a bit more information than not enough.

I think that it is safe to say that the Heinlein essay that I first read a few decades ago is as much the basis for this book as it was for my first book.

The subtitle of this book is "And the Inventions That They Inspired." To be perfectly accurate, perhaps I should have appended "Or Not" to the end of the subtitle. Not every case that I present in this book demonstrates that a story idea inspired an invention, although someone may have claimed that it did. I considered it equally important to demonstrate that a science fiction story idea was definitely not what inspired an invention.

Where I found it necessary to use material that has appeared in my first book, *The Great Heinlein Mystery,* or my second book, *An ASTOUNDING War*, I have attempted to provide additional information where it existed and to present the new version in what I hope is a more readable manner.

If some inventors have derived their inspiration from reading science fiction stories, how do other inventors get their ideas? This led me to look at a number of books that included *CREATIVITY: Flow and the Psychology of Discovery and Invention* by Mihaly Csikszentmihalyi, *INVENTology: How We Dream up Things That Change the World* by Pagan Kennedy, *JUICE: The Creative Fuel That Drives World-Class Inventors* by Evan I. Schwartz and *The Myths of Innovation* by Scott Berkun. I also hoped that I might encounter another case or two of inspiration by science fiction.

Although these and other books and a number of papers were interesting works on invention in general and some may have briefly mentioned science fiction, I did not encounter anything that helped me to find additional cases to investigate and analyze.

It was never my intent to simply throw a bunch of such cases at the reader. As you will see, I have devised a simple way of organizing the various cases that highlights their similarities and differences. And I have attempted to develop whatever conclusions are possible from the material

3

that was presented. While I hope that you will find what follows to be interesting, I also hope that it will stimulate you to see what you can discover on your own.

I had a bit of trouble with the title for this book, unlike my first two books. Early in my research for the first book, I wrote an article in an attempt to elicit information that could help me discover the answer. I called that article "The Great Heinlein Mystery." When it came time to name the first book, it was clear to me that I should just re-use the title of the article. The second book is a study of the connections between science fiction and World War II, with the focus on the magazine *Astounding Science-Fiction*. This quickly led me to *An ASTOUNDING War* as the best possible title.

For this book, I wanted to express a connection between ideas from science fiction and inventions. I made a long list of possible phrases and kept playing with different combinations. I did not want to just say "Science Fiction Ideas" and was not attracted to terms such as crazy, fantastic or outlandish. I asked both Jeff Mitchell and Gary Roen for their suggestions. I am grateful for their suggestions that led to my final choice for the title and subtitle.

Ed Wysocki
September 2018

1

INSPIRATION

Thinking about the connections between science fiction and inventions is nothing new.

James Osler Bailey (1903 – 1979), usually referred to as J. O. Bailey, received his A.B. degree from the University of North Carolina in 1924. In 1926, he began his graduate work in English. A discussion with his advisor, Professor H. M. Jones, led to him selecting the works of H. G. Wells as the topic for his master's essay. *The Scientific Novels of H.G Wells* was completed in 1927 and earned Bailey his M.A. degree. He then managed to convince the faculty that an expansion of his master's essay would make a good subject for the dissertation for his Ph.D.

Bailey completed the dissertation *Scientific Fiction in English, 1817-1914: A Study of Trends and Forms* and was awarded his Ph.D. in 1934. Ben Abramson was one of many people that he had contacted during the course of his research. He expressed an interest in possibly publishing Bailey's work. Acting on a suggestion from Abramson, Bailey expanded his dissertation to include material from after 1914. It was finally published by Argus Books in 1947 as *Pilgrims Through Space and Time: Trends and Patterns in Scientific and Utopian Fiction*.

At the time of Bailey's work, science fiction was not considered a topic suitable for study at the university level. Things have changed considerably in the years since his dissertation. The Science Fiction Research Association annually presents the Pilgrim Award for Lifetime Achievement in science fiction and fantasy scholarship, with the name taken from Bailey's book. The first award was made in 1970 to Bailey.

If you look at the bibliography in *Pilgrims*, you might see some familiar authors. Many works listed are from nineteenth century or even earlier. A number of the works of both Verne and Wells are listed. You will encounter *When Worlds Collide* and *After Worlds Collide* from the early 1930s. A few stories are from the pulp magazines *Amazing Stories* and *Astounding Stories*. The best-known work from the pulps that is listed is *The Skylark of Space* by E. E. "Doc" Smith. The latest listed work appears to be "Identity," a Venus Equilateral story by George O. Smith from the November 1945 issue of *Astounding Science-Fiction*. Since he mentioned George O. Smith, whose first story did not appear until October 1942, I have always wondered why Bailey did not also include authors such as Isaac Asimov, John W. Campbell, Jr. and Robert Heinlein.

In Chapter 1, Bailey presented his definition that:

> A piece of scientific fiction is a narrative of an imaginary invention or discovery in the natural sciences and consequent adventures and experiences.

This has always appeared to me to be a bit restrictive as a definition. Whether or not it is valid would depend on how much you wish to stretch the connection to an invention or discovery. For example, a tale of space travel would naturally involve some type of spaceship. One or more persons would have had to develop the engines and other components of the spaceship. Who they were, when they did it and how the spaceship actually works may not be relevant to the story at all. Does the mere existence of the spaceship place the story within the scope of Bailey's definition? In any case, his assertion set the tone for his book in presenting and analyzing all sorts of stories that fit his definition.

From my viewpoint, an important statement from *Pilgrims* appears in the chapter called "Invention and Discoveries." Bailey first wondered:

> It would be interesting to know whether any important invention has been inspired by an imaginary invention in fiction.

He conceded that works of imaginary invention have occurred during the time of experimentation in areas such as heavier-than-air flight or rocket propulsion but then made the statement that:

> *Even though a direct influence of imaginary invention upon actual invention can hardly be demonstrated,* the course of important inventions and discoveries in science fiction is worth record. (italics mine)

I had encountered Bailey's book and the above quote when I was doing my search to solve the Mystery of Heinlein's naval device. I realized that my efforts were in direct opposition to Bailey's statement.

In contrast with Bailey's statement that direct influence upon an invention cannot be shown, we may encounter people who seem intent on showing that practically everything was inspired by works of science fiction. An online search with the terms "science fiction" and "inventions" will lead you to a number of websites containing articles with titles that are some variation of "10 Inventions Inspired by Science Fiction."

In presenting the various claims made by people, I wish to illustrate the types of errors and pitfalls that may be encountered in trying to properly attribute the inspiration of inventions.

Since the word "inspired" is in the subtitle of the book as well as in the title of many of these websites or articles, let us look at its origin and how it is used.

The original meaning of inspire was one of motivation or guidance by a divine or supernatural influence. It may be traced back to the Latin *inspirare*, which means to blow into or breathe upon. The analogy is with blowing on a low flame to make it grow. In modern usage, inspire has a number of definitions. In the sense of a direct influence, an inspiration is the source of the idea behind some creative effort. This is the sense in which it is used in the title of this book and in the chapters that follow. In the sense of motivation, we could also say that a person may be inspired to perform work or study in a particular area or topic.

Consider the second definition, that of motivation. We have a statement from an essay by James Gunn:

> . . . scientists and explorers such as Igor Sikorsky, speleologist Norman Casteret, Admiral Richard Byrd, Lucius Beebe, Guglielmo Marconi, and Alberto Santos-Dumont credited Verne with inspiring their achievements. After a flight to the South Pole, Admiral Byrd said, "It was Jules Verne who launched me on this trip," and submarine developer Simon Lake began his autobiography with the words, "Jules Verne was in a sense the director general of my life."

Let us compare that statement with some items from an online Smithsonian article. The first three items listed are the Submarine, Helicopter and Rocket. The Submarine is associated with Simon Lake, the Helicopter with Igor Sikorsky and the Rocket with Robert H. Goddard.

Lake and Sikorsky are linked with works of Jules Verne and Goddard with H. G. Wells. What type of inspiration are we really seeing here?

Goddard may have been influenced by reading *The War of the Worlds* by Wells or even *From the Earth to the Moon* by Verne, but I can see nothing that would have suggested in any way the liquid fuel rocket. I do not believe that Sikorsky took anything definite from reading Verne's *Clipper of the Clouds* that led to his development of the first mass-produced helicopter.

The situation with Simon Lake is a bit confusing. On the basis of the above quote, one might be inclined to say that he was only referring to a general shaping of the path of his life. In his autobiography, however, Lake stated that he tried to improve on faults that he had identified in the fictional *Nautilus*. One example that he gave was the addition of an air-lock to the diving chamber.

The interpretation used in my research is that a person reads a work of science fiction and encounters a concept or a description of some device or system that serves as the <u>direct</u> inspiration for that person to proceed in the development of an invention.

There is another problem with some of the items that appear in these online lists. The person who has supplied the argument for certain items on a list of supposedly inspired inventions apparently did so with absolutely no knowledge of the facts.

To illustrate, an entry in another online article claims that the Global Positioning System (GPS) was based on *Star Trek*. This may be made clear by two statements:

> In 1995, thirty years after the concept debuted on *Star Trek*, the United States deemed a Global Positioning System a functional concept.

> On *Star Trek*, the Enterprise crew was located on the ground and beamed up by using GPS.

I was an avid watcher of the original *Star Trek* series and still watch the occasional episode that is being repeated 50 years later. After reading the above quotes, I tried without success to recall anything in an episode that one could remotely interpret as GPS. Locating Captain Kirk or some other member of the crew involved either locking onto their communicators or making use of the powerful but never explained suite of sensors available to Spock, Sulu, Chekov or some other member of the bridge crew.

Rather than depend on my personal recollection of the episodes, a better approach would be to give the real story of the origin of the GPS. This occurred in 1957 following the launch of Sputnik by the Soviet Union. Two scientists at the Applied Physics Laboratory (APL) of Johns Hopkins University, Drs. William Guier and George Weffenbach studied the orbit of the satellite. The satellite broadcast a continuous tone signal. The orbital motion of the satellite would cause a Doppler shift of the signal as it was received on the ground. They discovered that it was possible through analysis of the Doppler shift to determine the orbit of the satellite.

A colleague at APL then suggested an inversion of the problem. If you knew the position of the satellite, you could measure the signal and determine your own position on earth. This basic approach was implemented in what called the Navy Navigation Satellite System (also known as NAVSAT) using a small number of Transit satellites. This system was tested in 1960 and fully operational by 1964. Remember that the original *Star Trek* series did not appear on the air until 1966.

The Transit system had its limitations and the work in the years that followed was aimed at creating a system that was more accurate and easier to use. The first experimental GPS satellite was launched in 1978. I have encountered statements that say that GPS satellites are in geosynchronous orbits. This is not true; their positions are continually changing. Having more satellites in space means a better chance of having the required number of satellites visible at any time. In 1993, 24 GPS satellites were available, providing what was called Initial Operational Capability.

Each of the orbiting GPS satellites contains an atomic clock that is synchronized with a clock on the ground. The satellites are tracked from the ground and their positions are precisely known. When a GPS receiver picks up a signal from a satellite, the message is saying "I am at position X, and my time is T." The time it takes for the signal from a satellite to reach the receiver determines the distance to the satellite. By working with the signals from at least four satellites, the receiver is able to solve equations to determine a location that is consistent with the distances to each of the satellites.

I hope that the above discussion is sufficient to demonstrate that there was no connection at all between *Star Trek* and GPS. I will now use the above discussion as the incentive to briefly look at the possible influence of *Star Trek* on other technologies.

Let us begin with some of the more extreme *Star Trek* technologies, by which I mean phasers, transporter and warp drive. The phaser is just a variation of the ray gun known to science fiction for many years. The original pilot made use of a laser weapon, but the decision was then made to use a weapon with more impressive and unexplained capabilities. The transporter was developed purely as a means of getting the characters quickly on and off the ship without the need for costly and time-consuming scenes of transportation. There are so many technical problems associated with constructing and operating a transporter that one should not expect to see one soon, if ever.

The warp drive is just one technique used in science fiction to cope with the tremendous distances between stars. Over the years, authors have employed all sorts of imaginative ways of exceeding the speed of light. But then someone took a serious look at the problem. The theoretical physicist Miguel Alcubierre developed a speculative approach to faster than light travel based on the field equations of Einstein's theory of general relativity. The title of his original 1994 paper is "The warp drive: hyper-fast travel within general relativity." Without going into its principles of operation, let me simply say that it is not clear if it would ever be possible to construct such a system.

Let us now consider more mundane technologies appearing in *Star Trek*. It has been said by many people that the cell phone was inspired by the communicator in *Star Trek*. My answer to that claim has two parts. The first is that the concept of a portable telephone in science fiction occurred many years before *Star Trek*. To provide one such early example but not necessarily the earliest, I can point to *The 35th of May, or Conrad's Ride to the South Seas*, by Erich Kästner (1899 – 1974). You may not be familiar with Kästner, who was a German author. One of his later works, *Das doppelte Lottchen* (*The double Lottie*), is the story of two girls who meet at a summer camp and realize that they are identical twins separated by their divorced parents. If the plot sounds vaguely familiar, it was the basis for *The Parent Trap*.

The 35th of May, which first appeared in German in 1931, detailed the strange weekly adventures of a young boy Conrad with his uncle. During one adventure, they are in a city with moving sidewalks. A gentleman steps off the sidewalk, takes a phone from his pocket, calls his wife to say that he will be late for lunch, puts the phone back in his pocket and then steps back on the sidewalk. There are sufficient appearances of a portable telephone in other works of science fiction to show that it did not originate with *Star Trek*.

The second part of the answer requires that we look at the history of the cellular phone. The basic concept was put forth in a technical memo written by Douglas Ring at Bell Telephone Laboratories in 1947. In this memo, with the thrilling title "Mobile Telephony – Wide Area Coverage," Ring proposed an alternative to providing communications coverage to a large area from a central antenna. In his scheme, the large area would instead be divided into smaller areas. Although Ring did not use the word in his paper, these areas are what we now call *cells*. Within a cell, a particular set of frequencies would be used to establish a communications link with a mobile telephone. Such a link would only be valid for a short distance. When the telephone moved further from the antennas in its cell into an adjacent cell, it would then switch to a different set of frequencies. A small number of frequency sets could cover a large area since these sets could be used over and over again throughout the area.

Electronics technology had to develop and improve before it was possible to build a phone that would be light enough to carry and that would work for a reasonable amount of time before the batteries needed to be recharged. Martin Cooper of Motorola demonstrated a prototype cellular phone in 1973. In the television show *How William Shatner Changed the World*, Cooper stated that it was inspired by *Star Trek*. But there is a later interview on *Scene World Magazine* in which Cooper retracted that statement. He and his colleagues had been working on personal communications at Motorola for many years. If he was inspired by anything, Cooper said, it was possibly by Dick Tracy's wrist radio.

My opinion is that the only thing about the cellular phones that was inspired by *Star Trek* was the packaging of certain models. In 1989, Motorola introduced the MicroTac, in which the mouthpiece section folded up over the keyboard. The StarTac, which appeared in 1996, was the first clamshell / flip phone. There is no doubt that it strongly resembles the communicator used in the original series.

Now consider the Tricorder. This was a device that was proposed by Gene Roddenberry, the creator of the original *Star Trek* series. The tricorder and other props for *Star Trek*, including the communicator, were designed and constructed by Wah Ming Chang. The "tri" part of name was meant signify the three functions of sensing, recording and computing. Versions of the tricorder would have been used by crew members for engineering purposes on board the *Enterprise* or to gather data during missions away from the ship. The best-known version, however, was the medical tricorder employed by Doctor McCoy.

Since the fictional tricorder appeared, various companies or university researchers have used the name for devices, including a spectrometer and a DNA analyzer. Here I will only consider the Tricorder XPrize. In an XPrize competition, a goal is established that will force the competitors to develop innovative ideas and approaches. A particular competition is defined by its goals, deadlines and the prizes awarded to the winners.

The very first XPrize was for suborbital flight. The goal was to develop a spaceship carrying three people that would be able to reach outer space (higher than 100 km.) and fly two times within two weeks. The prize of $10 million was won in 2004 by the Tier One project of Burt Rutan's company Scaled Composites, which was funded by Paul Allen (co-founder of Microsoft).

In 2012, the Tricorder XPrize Competition was announced. Sponsored by the Qualcomm Foundation, its objective was to address problems that exist in healthcare. In addition to problems with cost and access, many people do not receive the recommended screening, diagnosis or treatment.

As originally defined, the winner of the $10 million Tricorder XPrize would be required to assess a set of sixteen distinct conditions and five vital signs. The system capable of performing all of the required functions had to weigh no more than five pounds. The system had to operate in a non-invasive manner and be able to be operated without the assistance of a medical professional.

The original core set of thirteen conditions included anemia, diabetes, stroke, tuberculosis, pneumonia and absence of core conditions. Absence of core conditions meant that the individual is free of all of the core conditions as well as three chosen from the elective set of conditions. The elective set consisted of ten items which included hypertension, airborne allergens, mononucleosis, shingles, strep throat and HIV screen. The five vital signs are blood pressure, electrocardiography, body temperature, respiratory rate and oxygen saturation. The requirements were later modified to remove stroke, tuberculosis and hepatitis A from the core set and airborne allergens and osteoporosis from the elective set.

From the many teams that applied, ten teams were selected for the competition. Four of the teams were from the United States; the other teams were from Canada, India, Taiwan, Slovenia, UK and Ireland.

The competition was concluded in April 2017. No team met all of the requirements for the grand prize. Final Frontier Medical Devices (US) was awarded $2.6 million and Dynamical Biomarkers Group (Taiwan) was awarded $1 million. Cloud DX (Canada) was named "Bold Epic Innovator" and awarded $100,000. Some of the unawarded prize money will be used for further development and consumer testing.

I had originally considered including the Tricorder among the cases to be considered in later chapters. The first reason I did not is that it was a competition among many teams rather than the inspiration of one person by a story idea. The second reason is that the story of the medical tricorder is not yet complete.

We may not have heard the last of the XPrize with regard to science fiction and inventions. If you look at a list of the various XPrize competitions, the one involving the Tricorder is the only one so far with a direct connection to science fiction. On the XPrize website, however, there is a page that refers to a Science Fiction Advisory Council (https://www.xprize.org/about/scifi). All that the page really says is that the members of the Council "will lend their expertise in honing our vision of the future." This strikes me as a somewhat vague description of what is expected, but perhaps this will create a new link between science fiction and inventions in the years to come.

I would like to close my discussion of items related to Star Trek by presenting a case that points to the need to pay attention to dates. This case refers to the movie *Star Trek IV: The Voyage Home*. A gigantic alien spacecraft has arrived at Earth and is transmitting a signal of such power that it is disrupting Earth's climate and technologies. Spock identifies the signal as the song of humpback whales. As humpbacks are extinct in the time of *Star Trek*, the only way to save the Earth is for the members of the crew to travel in time back to 1986 and return with humpback whales to respond to the signal.

In 1986, the crew makes plans to take the whales aboard the captured Klingon ship that they are using. It is necessary to construct a tank to hold the whales and water for the return trip. Scotty and McCoy contact a manufacturer to have him construct the material for the tanks and as payment they provide him with the secret of "transparent aluminum."

There does exist a material that is sometimes called transparent aluminum. It is very strong and optically transparent over a range that includes visible light. One might conclude that it was inspired by the movie. Let me first state that the name is somewhat misleading. It is not possible for a metal to be transparent to visible light. It is possible, however, for ceramics to be transparent. Aluminum Oxynitride is a ceramic that is composed of aluminum, oxygen and nitrogen.

The application for the patent "Transparent aluminum oxynitride and method of manufacture" was made in 1984 and issued in 1985 as U.S. patent 4,520,116. There are other patents regarding aluminum oxynitride as early as 1980. Since *Star Trek IV* did not appear until 1986, it is more reasonable to assume that knowledge of the real substance led to be it being used in the movie under the name of transparent aluminum.

Another way in which a science fiction story may be connected to a real invention is by name only. In the Smithsonian article, there is an entry for the Waldo. A story named "Waldo" by Robert Heinlein (as Anson MacDonald) appeared in the August 1942 issue of *Astounding Science-Fiction*. This story will also be discussed in Chapter 7. Waldo Jones suffered from a disease that greatly reduced the strength of his muscles. He lived in zero gravity in an orbiting station and developed remote manipulators to amplify the efforts of his muscles.

In the quest to develop to develop the atomic bomb during World War II, the Manhattan Project, it was necessary to work with highly radioactive materials. This could be done only at a distance and from behind thick lead shielding, using mechanical manipulators. Someone among the scientists and engineers called the manipulators "waldos" after Heinlein's story. Although the entry for Waldos appears on the Smithsonian article on inspired inventions, it does not claim that it was the inspiration for the real-life device.

Another entry on the same page was for the TASER. It states correctly the acronym stands for Thomas A. Swift's Electric Rifle. The actual work by Victor Appleton was *Tom Swift and his Electric Rifle or Daring Inventions in Elephant Land*. It appears that the "A" was added to make the acronym pronounceable. As was the case with the Waldo, it is not claimed that the device was inspired by the story. According to the obituary of its inventor, Jack Cover, the inspiration for the TASER was from a newspaper story of a person who was "frozen" by coming into contact with electrified fence but survived the experience. The weapon in the Tom Swift story projected a dangerous and destructive electric charge. This is quite different from the TASER's purpose of safely immobilizing a person.

The final case is that of the credit card. The term comes from *Looking Backward From 2000 to 1887* by Edward Bellamy. It employed the Rip Van Winkle plot device where a character sleeps for many years, emerging into a greatly changed society. In Bellamy's story, the reader is presented with the United States of 2000 as a socialist utopia.

Every citizen is provided a yearly stipend as his share of the annual product of the nation. This card is used to make the purchase of whatever the person desires from the public warehouses. Although the word credit is used in the sense of the value distributed to each citizen, the system operates by deducting from the value initially placed on the card. Based on current usage, we would call it a debit card. Specialized charging systems for purchases in department stores or travel by air appeared in the first half of the twentieth century. The first general purpose credit card, Diners Club, did not appear until 1950.

In this chapter, I have attempted to show the various problems that may be encountered when discussing science fiction and inventions. I have done my best to avoid such problems in the chapters that follow.

2

SIMILARITY

I have been able to collect information about various inventions and their apparent connection with works of science fiction. My first problem was in finding some means of organizing their presentation to the reader.

Cases have been encountered that claimed inspiration by science fiction but were based solely on the fact that the invention looked like or performed a function similar to something that appeared in a story. No other information was supplied to support such an assertion. This suggested the first step in organizing the inventions that I will present. The term to be used is, quite logically, SIMILARITY. You see or hear of an invention and you say to yourself, "That's sounds like something in a science fiction story by Heinlein (or Asimov, or Clarke, or . . .)." No more, no less.

Now consider everything else you might be able to discover about the invention, the inventor, the story and the author. Anything that would be able to help you establish a connection or lack of connection between the invention and the story. The most obvious name for the collection of such material is EVIDENCE.

SIMILARITY and EVIDENCE are totally separate and distinct from one another. One does not affect the other.

Now that we have two such concepts, what do we do with them? Here is where an engineering background becomes useful. Upon the completion of some experiment or test, you usually have a collection of data points. You want to know if there is some pattern or relationship indicated by the data. The first step in such an analysis is to plot the data points. The manner in which the data is plotted depends on the nature of the experiment. Whatever approach is taken, you hope that the plot will tell you something useful. In some cases, the plotted points may fall on or near a particular curve. In other cases, you may see what appears to be a random scattering of data points. Such an approach makes use of the ability of the human mind to see patterns in collections of objects.

Here we do not have numerical data points to plot, but some form of a graphical approach still seemed to me to be the way to proceed.

So how do we begin? We are bound to encounter varying degrees of similarity between inventions and stories. Therefore, we define one line as the SIMILARITY axis, with No Similarity at one end and Identical at the other end. Then we will find varying degrees of evidence, so we define an EVIDENCE axis. If these two axes meet at a right angle, the usual arrangement, we would have the simple form of a plot in the form of the letter L. It is extremely important to realize that we can have two types of evidence – evidence FOR the story having inspired the invention and evidence AGAINST the story having inspired the invention. For example, a bit of research might reveal that the invention actually came before the story. That would count as very strong evidence against, don't you think?

This would result in a plot in the shape of an inverted capital T, as shown in Figure 1.

The solid vertical line in the center is the SIMILARITY axis, with No Similarity at its point of intersection with the horizontal axis and Identical at the top. A dotted horizontal line at the top just extends the rating of Identical to the left and the right.

The solid horizontal line at the bottom is the EVIDENCE axis. At the center where it intersects with the SIMILARITY axis, we have zero evidence to support either assertion regarding inspiration. At each extreme right and left, we have absolute certainty FOR or AGAINST. This could arise from a large collection of evidence that leaves absolutely no doubt at all or could be as simple as a statement by the inventor that he or she either was or was not inspired by the story in question. Absolute certainty is indicated by the vertical dotted lines at either end of the EVIDENCE axis.

I will call this plot, for obvious reasons, the SIMILARITY-EVIDENCE plot, or S-E plot.

This is not meant to be a graph where numerical values are to be plotted. I am not going to introduce any mathematical formulas by which numerical values representing the degree of similarity or amount of evidence might be calculated and then plotted. The S-E plot is at most a means of organizing and visualizing the cases I will be presenting.

In each case, there will be an Invention A that appears to be related to story X. I will create a point to represent the pair (A, X) and place it somewhere on the S-E plot. The location of the point is my choice, based

Figure 1. The S-E Plot.

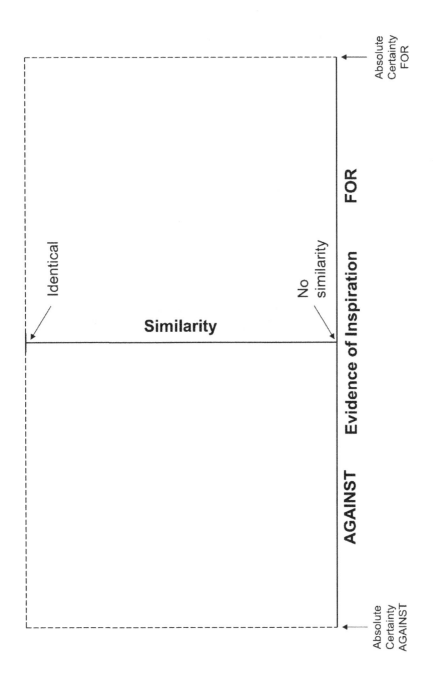

on the degree of similarity and strength of the evidence. It is entirely subjective. If two such points are placed close together on the S-E plot, someone is bound to say that the evidence in one case is stronger than the other, so its point should be closer to the certainty line. Or that the degree of similarity in one case is stronger than the other, so its point should be higher up. I will state now that I absolutely refuse to be drawn into such discussions or arguments.

Let us assume that you have heard of an invention B and feel that it is similar to something from a science fiction story Y. Create a new point that we will call (B, Y). Where do you place that point? If you know nothing else other than the perceived similarity, you have no choice but to place this point directly on the SIMILARITY axis. How high or low on the axis is up to you. Until you can begin to collect evidence of any kind, the point remains on the vertical axis. Once you begin to collect such evidence, however, the point can begin to move either left or right according to the nature of the evidence.

We could create many points that remain on the SIMILARITY axis. These will represent cases where evidence cannot be discovered. The lack of evidence does not mean that the invention was definitely not inspired by the story. You would need evidence to support the assertion that it was not inspired just as much as you would need evidence to support the assertation that it was inspired.

After I have presented the results of my research for each of the cases that I have found, I will discuss their proposed placement on the S-E chart.

3

A NEUTRAL POSITION

The problem was in getting power from the atom.

Let us begin by looking at a work of fiction, *The Crack of Doom*. This novel was written by Robert Cromie, a Belfast journalist and novelist, and was published in 1895. A secret society, headed by a gentleman named Herbert Brande, has a plan to destroy the world using the great power contained in matter. A demonstration in the Mediterranean of the energy obtained from a very small amount of matter results in the unintended destruction of a group of French fishing boats. The gigantic explosion is to be set off on an island in the Arafura Sea, north of Australia. Through the actions of the hero, the actual blast does not possess the world-shattering power that Brande had intended. The book ends with the fate of a parallel expedition to Labrador unknown.

Where did Cromie get the idea for the release of large amounts of energy from matter? As the discovery of radioactivity revealed that at least some elements possessed previously unknown stores of energy, one might be inclined to say that radioactivity was what inspired Cromie. I have found at least one author who has made that claim. The discovery of radioactivity in uranium by Henri Becquerel, however, did not occur until 1896, the year after Cromie's work was published.

Today, we know that great amounts of energy may be obtained from either nuclear fission or fusion. In any discussion of these processes, we encounter the equation $E = mc^2$ that tells us the energy that may be obtained from any amount of matter. This equation is attributed to the physicist Albert Einstein.

As it turns out, Einstein was not the first to make such a derivation. His calculations were performed on the basis of his theory of relativity. There were other earlier similar derivations based on the theory of the existence of the ether. The ether was proposed to explain how light waves could travel through empty space. As time passed, however, problems developed with the necessary properties of the ether. Since it filled all of space, ether could not slow down the planets in their orbits, which meant that it had to be a massless fluid. At the same time, it would have to be very rigid to support the propagation of light waves. It was finally possible to explain observations and physical phenomena without making use of the ether and its conflicting properties.

One ether-based derivation of the relationship between energy and matter was made by Samuel Preston, a British engineer and physicist. He assumed that the universe was filled with ether particles moving at the speed of light. In his book, *Physics of the Ether*, which was published in 1875, he stated that:

> A quantity of matter representing a mass of one grain endued with the velocity of the ether particles, encloses an amount of energy which, if entirely utilized, would be competent to project a weight of one hundred thousand tons to a height of nearly two miles (1.9 miles).

Did Cromie use Preston's work as the basis for his story? We need only look at the end of Chapter II where the villain Brande is explaining the amount of energy that may be obtained from the atom:

> "If you will consult a common text-book on the *physics of the ether*," he replied, "you will find that one grain of matter contains sufficient energy, if etherised, to raise a hundred thousand tons nearly two miles." (italics mine)

A comparison of the quotes should leave no doubt that Cromie got the idea from Preston. Although he referred to a "common text-book," he managed to sneak in the title of Preston's book.

One question is, what was actually happening in physics in the years after the publication of Cromie's novel?

In 1896, Henri Becquerel discovered that previously unknown radiation was emitted by minerals that contained the element uranium.

At that time, nothing at all was known about the structure of the atom. The first step in understanding this structure occurred in 1897 with the discovery of the electron by J. J. Thomson. Aside from being the fundamental unit of electricity, it was also realized that electrons were among the components of every atom.

The year 1898 was a year of many advances in the area of radioactivity by Marie and Pierre Curie. Marie Curie began by investigating certain minerals that contained uranium. She found that the minerals were more active than the uranium. In the course of her investigations, it was discovered that a known element, thorium, was also radioactive. Working with her husband Pierre, it was discovered that this additional activity in the minerals was due to two new radioactive elements. The discovery of these two elements, which were given the names polonium and radium, was announced in 1898.

While new radioactive elements were being discovered and studied, there was also work into the nature of the radiation that was being emitted. In 1899, Ernest Rutherford detected two distinct forms of radiation, which he named alpha and beta rays. The following year Paul Villard discovered an even more penetrating form of radiation that he called gamma rays.

In 1900, Henri Becquerel was able to establish that the beta ray was actually a particle and was also able to show that it was Thomson's electron. The same year, Rutherford discovered that a radioactive gas was given off by the element thorium. This had also been observed by Marie and Pierre Curie in their work with radium. Rutherford put the chemist Frederick Soddy to work to determine the nature of the gas. Based on the analysis, it was concluded that the thorium was transmuting into an inert gas. This was another new element that was eventually given the name radon.

We know from history of the efforts of alchemists who tried to convert metals such as lead into gold. As the various elements became known and the principles of chemistry developed during the nineteenth century, it was generally accepted that such transmutation was not possible.

It was then discovered that the basis of radioactivity was the spontaneous transmutation of radioactive elements. This transmutation occurs by the emission of either alpha or beta particles. The result of the transmutation may either be a different element or a different form of the original element. Different forms of the same element are called isotopes, a term which is credited to Soddy. Another key discovery by Rutherford and Soddy was that a radioactive isotope of any element possesses a value called its half-life. This is the time for half of the atoms of that isotope to transmute. This enabled the results of transmutation – radioactive decay – to be detected and identified.

In 1907, Rutherford was able to demonstrate that an alpha particle was actually the nucleus of a helium atom. The nucleus will be discussed later in this chapter. The principle behind his demonstration was very simple, as many great demonstrations are. A glass tube was made with very thin walls. This tube was then filled with radon, the radioactive gas emitted by radium. Radon was known to emit alpha particles. This tube was then surrounded by a second tube from which the air was evacuated. Alpha particles passed through the thin inner tube and collected in the space between the tubes. After a period of time, analysis was performed that revealed that the space between the tubes contained helium.

We now come to a very important book. This was *The Interpretation of Radium* by Frederick Soddy, which was published in 1908. This book was based on a series of six lectures delivered at the University of Glasgow that same year. Soddy's intent, as explained in the Preface, was to help the lay reader understand the discoveries that had been made and their significance. The lecture material was modified to account for the absence of the demonstrations performed during the lectures, but also included the latest results obtained by Rutherford, Hans Geiger and Soddy.

Soddy's book is divided into eleven chapters. The first ten chapters clearly and logically discussed the energy given off by radium, uranium and thorium. The radioactive emissions—alpha, beta and gamma rays—were discussed. Then the process of transmutation of elements was explored for both radium and uranium.

The most important chapter from our viewpoint is the last, Chapter XI. Soddy pointed out that radium seems so wonderful because it is changing rapidly in comparison with uranium. He wondered if the store of energy was restricted to just radioactive elements and suggested that it was not. Three important statements made by Soddy should be noted. First, he considered the process of extracting energy from uranium:

> This bottle contains about one pound of uranium oxide, and therefore about fourteen ounces of uranium. Its value is about £ 1. Is it not wonderful to reflect that in this little bottle there lies asleep and waiting to be evolved the energy of about nine hundred tons of coal? The energy in a ton of uranium would be sufficient to light London for a year. The store of energy in uranium would be worth a thousand times as much as the uranium itself, if only it were under our control and could be harnessed to do the world's work in the same way as the stored energy in coal has been harnessed and controlled.

How could this be accomplished?

> . . . to increase the natural rate, and to break down uranium or any other element artificially, is simply transmutation. If we could accomplish the one so we could the other. These two great problems, at once the oldest and the newest in science, are one.

Transmutation of the elements carries with it the power to unlock the internal energy of matter, and the unlocking of the internal stores of energy in matter would, strangely enough, be infinitely the most important and valuable consequence of transmutation.

And what would be the results of such transmutation?

... if it were possible artificially to disintegrate an element with a heavier atom than gold and produce gold from it, so great an amount of energy would probably be evolved that the gold in comparison would be of little account. The energy would be far more valuable than the gold.

The importance of these statements will be clear when we consider a work of fiction created by Herbert George Wells in 1913.

When the name of H. G. Wells (1866 – 1946) is mentioned, most people will think of him only as an author of science fiction. In fact, he wrote more than science fiction, or as they would have been called, "scientific romances." He wrote essays and books on a range of political and social topics as well as a number of more conventional novels. For those with an interest in the details of his life, you might consider either *H. G. Wells: Desperately Mortal* by David Smith or *H. G. Wells: Another Kind of Life* by Michael Sherborne.

Stories by Wells, both science fiction or not, appeared in print as early as 1887. His science fiction novels began with *The Time Machine* in 1895. Other science fiction novels in the years that followed included *The Island of Dr. Moreau* (1896), *The Invisible Man* (1897), *The War of the Worlds* (1898) and *The First Men in the Moon* (1901).

During the first decade of the twentieth century, other novels by Wells began to appear. *Kipps* (1905) was a study in class differences. *Ann Veronica* (1909) was the story of the rebellion of a young woman against the stern rule of her father. *The History of Mr. Polly* (1910) was drawn from the experiences of Wells in the drapery trade.

From 1908, when *The War in the Air* appeared, the only work of science fiction by Wells that appeared until 1914 was *The Sleeper Awakes* (1910). This was a revision of *When the Sleeper Wakes*, which was published in 1899.

Then in 1914, there appeared *The World Set Free*. Wells began work on this novel in early 1913 while staying at Chateau Soleil in Randogne, Switzerland. The chateau was the home of Elizabeth von Arnim, who was the mistress of Wells from 1910 to 1913.

A close friend of Wells, dating from their days at the Normal School of Science (later the Royal College of Science) was A. T. "Tommy" Simmons. In a letter to Simmons, Wells referred to this new work:

I've suddenly broken out into one of the good old scientific romances again. And I suddenly need to know quite the latest about the atomic theory and sources of energy.

The primary source of information for Wells in constructing this work was Frederick Soddy, through his book *The Interpretation of Radium* and by personal contact. The dedication to *The World Set Free* is "To Frederick Soddy's '*The Interpretation of Radium*'." The dedication also made specific reference to Chapter XI, which contained Soddy's speculations.

The World Set Free consists of a Prelude and five long chapters.

Most of the Prelude is taken up with a discussion of how man progressed from a savage to the level of civilization at the beginning of the twentieth century. Part of the discussion of this progress concerned the sources of power that had been developed, culminating with steam and electricity. The end of the Prelude presents a lecture being given by a Professor Rufus in Edinburgh.

You may recall that Soddy's book was based on lectures delivered in Glasgow. It seems clear by the content of Rufus's lecture that he is meant to represent Soddy. He refers to small bottle of uranium oxide in a way that leaves no doubt that the source is the first quote from Soddy's book presented above. The professor also speaks of what would happen if the rate of disintegration could be increased. This also comes from Soddy's book and is the key to the technology presented in the chapter that follows.

In the first chapter "The New Source of Energy," we find that Holsten, who was briefly introduced in the Prelude, showed that it was possible to release energy from one of the heavy elements. Instead of uranium or thorium, the element chosen by Wells for the source of energy was bismuth. In line with the last of the quotes taken from Soddy's book, it is stated that the final result of the process that began with bismuth was gold.

Holsten's discovery was placed in 1933, but Wells has another twenty years pass before the process is brought to industrial application as the Holsten-Roberts engine. Other similar processes soon followed: Dass-Tata, Kemp and Krupp-Erlanger.

In the rest of Chapter I, we are presented with effects that the release of energy from the atom has upon society. The automobile was replaced by a lighter vehicle that cost practically nothing to operate. If you did not wish to travel on the roads, it was possible to fly in an aircraft capable of both horizontal and high-speed vertical fight.

The creation of gold as the result of operating the atomic engines has a destabilizing effect upon the economy. With the removal of the demand for coal and oil, these industries collapsed. Other industries were affected as well and large numbers of workers found themselves unemployed. A more personal look at the economic and social effects of atomic power was presented through the character Frederick Barnet, an educated and prosperous man whose family fortune was destroyed.

We then come to the second chapter "The Last War." Of interest to us here are the atomic bombs that were employed. They were small enough to be dropped by hand from airplanes. The description of the action of the bombs in *The World Set Free* is totally unlike what we know as an atomic bomb. Instead of the energy being released within a fraction of a second, the reaction continues for days. The description of the principle behind the bombs is doubletalk of the highest order:

> Those used by the allies were lumps of pure Carolinum, painted on the outside with unoxidized cydonator inducive enclosed hermetically in a case of membranium. A little celluloid stud between the handles by which the bomb was lifted was arranged so as to be easily torn off and admit air to the inducive, which at once became active and set up radioactivity in the outer layer of the Carolinum sphere. This liberated fresh inducive, and so in a few minutes the whole bomb was a blazing continual explosion.

This chapter concludes with the experiences of Frederick Barnet during the war.

The rest of the book is concerned with the efforts made after the war to set up a World Republic. These chapters only serve as a place for Wells to employ some of his social and political theories and are of no real interest to us here.

Now we will consider the man who was led, at least in part, to his invention by his reading of *The World Set Free*.

Leo Szilard (1898 – 1954) was born in Budapest in the Kingdom of Hungary, which was part of the Austro-Hungarian Empire. He was actually born as Leo Spitz, the surname likely assumed by his paternal ancestors upon settling in Slovakia. In 1900, in response to a government policy, the German name Spitz was changed to Szilard, which means "solid" in Hungarian.

Leo soon gained a brother Bela in 1900 and a sister Rose in 1901. He was quite an extraordinary child. He spoke and read French and German by the time he was six. He read well above the level normal for a child his age. He had a talent for math, often arriving at unconventional solutions.

All of the Szilard children received home schooling by a tutor from ages six through nine. At the age of ten Leo entered what was called a practical or real school. This type of school taught science and technology, as opposed to a gymnasium, which taught classical subjects. This was driven by the decision of Leo's father that he should become an engineer.

While he was still in school, World War I broke out with the Austro-Hungarian Empire aligned with Germany. In January 1916, Leo received a telegram assigning him to the Fifth Fortress Regiment. He was allowed to graduate from high school in June 1916 and begin his studies in the fall at the Palatine Joseph Technical University (now Budapest Technical University).

A year later, in September 1917, Leo Szilard became a member of the Fourth Mountain-Artillery Regiment. Instead of a posting to some location in the field, he was assigned to Reserve Officer School. This was located in Budapest, which enabled him to visit his family.

In May 1918, Leo finally found himself with his regiment at a camp near Innsbruck, Austria. In September, 1918 he became very ill and managed to obtain a leave of absence to go home to Budapest. Once there, he was admitted to an army hospital where the diagnosis was Spanish influenza. He later learned that his regiment had been in combat and all of his comrades had disappeared. The influenza had saved his life.

The war came to an end on November 11, 1918 and Leo was soon a civilian again. Although he resumed his studies at the University, the political situation in Hungary soon intervened.

The Austro-Hungarian empire collapsed and Hungary declared itself an independent republic with Count Mihály Károlyi as Prime Minister. Leo and his brother Bela had joined other students in political discussions drifting into socialism. The universities were briefly closed at the end of 1918 and when they reopened Leo and Bela again resumed their studies.

The Károyli government was succeeded in March 1919 by the Hungarian Soviet Republic, led by Béla Kun. Its excesses led to its collapse on August 1. It was soon followed by the government of Austro-Hungarian Admiral Miklós Horthy, which lasted until 1944.

Following the fall of the Kun regime, in September 1919, both Leo and Bela tried to register at the University but were beaten and forced away because they were Jews. When Leo then tried to obtain permission to study abroad, however, the Horthy government refused on the basis of his socialist activities under the Kun regime. Making use of connections through trusted friends and some bribes, Leo was able to obtain a passport. He had to leave Hungary between December 25, 1919 and January 5,

1920.

He arrived in Berlin on January 6, 1920 and succeeded in registering at the Technische Hochschule of Berlin. He was soon joined by Bela, who had convinced the government to let him study abroad as well.

Leo soon lost interest in engineering and decided to switch to physics. This required a change to the Friedrich Wilhelm University. He continued taking courses at the Technische Hochschule and began the process of applying to the University. It was not until October 1920 that he was finally admitted.

In the course of my research, I discovered two interesting stories from Szilard's life. The first involved his activities as a student. To obtain a Ph.D., it was necessary to submit a thesis that involved original scientific work. The topic could be suggested by the student or a professor. Leo chose as his thesis adviser Max von Laue who had received the 1914 Nobel Prize in Physics for the discovery of X-ray diffraction by crystals.

The topic suggested by von Laue concerned Einstein's Theory of Relativity. In addition to his research at the Kaiser Wilhelm Institute, Albert Einstein also gave a weekly seminar at the University. Szilard asked Einstein to teach him and a few friends the concepts of statistical mechanics. These friends included three Hungarians: Eugene Wigner, John von Neumann and Dennis Gabor. We can measure certain quantities such as the temperature or pressure of some physical system. Statistical mechanics relates these quantities to the behavior of the microscopic components of the system. To do so, it makes use of statistical methods and probability theory.

After working for several months, Szilard felt that he could not solve the problem posed by von Laue. He was not even sure that a solution was possible. During the university holiday in December 1921, he decided to stop work on his thesis problem and take a break. As he took long walks during December, he began to think about something very distant from his thesis topic.

Szilard began to think about how to reconcile apparent differences between the classic physics of Newton and the newer physics based on the work of Max Planck. The problem that he considered was in the area of thermodynamics. The Second Law of Thermodynamics states that it is impossible for heat to be spontaneously transferred from a cold body to a hotter body.

There were two views of the problem of thermodynamic equilibrium. The phenomenological approach was based on the principle that heat flows from hot to cold regions. This could be demonstrated by many types of experiments. The statistical approach involved models of large numbers of atomic particles involving the use of statistics and probability. Over the course of three weeks of walking and thinking during the day and then writing the results down each evening, he found a way to reconcile the two approaches.

With a manuscript in hand, he was reluctant to take it to von Laue as it was not the problem he had been assigned. He decided to present his work to Einstein and ask for his advice. When he explained his result, Einstein's first reaction was that it was impossible. After Szilard explained what he had done in more detail, Einstein accepted his solution. This led him to present the work to von Laue. He told him that it was not the problem he had been assigned but wondered if it could be accepted as the topic for his dissertation. The next morning, he received a telephone call from von Laue who said, "Your manuscript has been accepted as your thesis for your Ph.D. degree." The title of his thesis was "On the Manifestation of Thermodynamic Fluctuations."

During the 1920s and into the 1930s, Szilard came up with a number of ideas but did little to develop them. These included the electron microscope, a linear particle accelerator and even a cyclotron. One exception was a refrigerator based on a liquid metal coolant circulated by an electromagnetic pump with no moving parts. Szilard developed this in conjunction with Einstein. A model of the refrigerator was built and several patents were filed for the pump. The refrigerator was not practical; the pump design found application years later in nuclear reactors that employed a liquid metal coolant. For a time, Szilard also served as von Laue's assistant.

Szilard received German citizenship in 1930 as a consequence of his position as a *Privatdocent* (University lecturer) at the University of Berlin. By 1933, with the rise of Hitler, Germany was changing in ways that were worrying to Szilard. This brings us to the second interesting Szilard story.

On January 30, 1933, Adolf Hitler was named Chancellor of Germany. The evening of February 27, there occurred the destruction of the Reichstag building by fire, which Hitler blamed on the Communists. On March 23, Hitler proposed a law that transferred the powers of the Reichstag to his cabinet. This was followed by the proposal of a boycott against Jewish businesses and the restriction of Jews in the universities and the professions in proportion to their numbers in the population of Germany.

On March 30, Szilard finally decided to leave Germany. He took his two bags and proceeded to the train station where he bought a one-way first-class ticket on the night train to Vienna. Very few people were taking the train that evening. He fell asleep during the journey and was awakened by a police officer in the morning at the border between Germany and Czechoslovakia. The officer asked for his papers.

What did this officer see? He saw a well-dressed gentleman in his mid-30s whose papers indicated that he was on the faculty of the University of Berlin. And this gentleman was travelling in first-class. This choice of first-class was made by Szilard since he liked to travel in style, but also because he thought that it would make him less likely to be interrogated. As he had hoped, the officer asked only a few questions, returned his papers and let him proceed. Szilard had been concerned about the possibility of his luggage being searched since it contained a number of bundles of currency. Later that morning, the train arrived in Vienna.

It is necessary to mention a postscript to Szilard's journey. The next evening, the same train was full as a result of the start of the anti-Jewish boycott. Everyone on the train was questioned; some were not allowed to proceed or their possessions were seized. Szilard later made light of his close call by saying:

> This just goes to show that if you want to succeed in this world you don't have to be much cleverer than other people, you just have to be one day earlier.

Before proceeding, I must say a few things about the advances in the knowledge of the structure of the nucleus since the publication of *The Interpretation of Radium* and *The World Set Free*.

As of 1897, the electron was known to be a component of every atom. Since an atom is electrically neutral, this meant that the negative charge of all of the electrons had to be balanced by a positive charge of equal magnitude. The question was how the positive charge existed in the atom. In 1904, J. J. Thomson proposed a model in which the electrons were distributed within a region of the required positive charge. This became known as the plum pudding model.

This is where matters stood until experiments were performed by firing alpha particles at thin gold foils. The results were not consistent with the plum pudding model and could only be explained if the positive charge was concentrated in a very small nucleus and was surrounded by the electrons. By 1917, it was established that the single positive charge of the hydrogen nucleus was also present in the nuclei of other elements. This unit of positive charge was given the name proton.

With only the electron and proton to work with, however, there were problems in coming up with a reasonable model of the nucleus.

The atomic number, which is the number of protons within the nucleus (or the number of electrons surrounding the nucleus), corresponds to the position of the element within the periodic table. Hydrogen is 1, helium is

2, lithium is 3, and so on up to uranium, which is 92. Then there is the atomic weight. If we consider the more common isotopes of certain elements, the atomic weight of helium is 4, lithium is 7 and uranium is either 235 or 238. How does one account for the difference between the two numbers?

One proposal was that there were additional protons within the nucleus to make up the difference between the atomic number and the atomic weight. If that was done, however, a way had to be found to neutralize the positive charge of these additional protons. To do this, it was also necessary to place a number of electrons within the nucleus. There were, unfortunately, a number of problems connected with the presence of electrons within the nucleus. The maximum size of a nucleus was known and it might not be possible to fit all of the needed electrons. Other problems arose from the new field of quantum mechanics. Another solution had to be found.

The difficulty was resolved by the neutron. This is a particle with the same mass as the proton but with no electric charge. The neutron was first proposed in a talk given by Ernest Rutherford in June 1920. It is one thing to propose a new subatomic particle. It is quite another matter to show that such a particle actually exists.

Experiments had been performed in which alpha particles were directed onto various elements. For elements near the start of the periodic table, such as lithium or beryllium, this caused a very penetrating radiation to be emitted. When this radiation obtained from beryllium was directed onto paraffin, it caused protons to be emitted. One interpretation was that the new radiation was composed of gamma rays.

James Chadwick did not believe that interpretation. In early 1932, he began by repeating the earlier experiments and was able to show that the gamma ray explanation was not acceptable. Gamma rays would not have sufficient energy to dislodge protons. He went on to show that the radiation could be explained if it consisted of neutral particles as had been proposed by Rutherford in 1920. Experiments by others confirmed the existence of the neutron as a new fundamental particle. For his discovery, Chadwick received the Nobel Prize in Physics in 1935.

So now we have three subatomic particles: the electron, the proton and the neutron. The atomic weight of an element is then given by the sum of the number of protons and the number of neutrons within the nucleus. All of the different isotopes of a given element have the same number of protons, but each isotope has a different number of neutrons. One extremely useful feature of the neutron is that it can be used to probe the nucleus as it is not affected by its positive charge.

We now have all we need to return to the story of Leo Szilard.

After leaving Germany, Szilard established his base in London, although he travelled extensively through Europe. Most of his efforts were devoted to finding ways to assist other refugee scholars. In the area of science, he began to develop an interest in biology. He was then drawn back into physics.

On September 11, 1933 Ernest Rutherford delivered a talk at the annual meeting of the British Association for the Advancement of Science. Szilard was ill with a cold that day and was unable to attend. He had to be satisfied with reading the report on Rutherford's talk that appeared in *The Times* the next day.

The summary of the talk concluded with the statement by Rutherford that "anyone who looked for a source of power in the transformation of atoms was talking moonshine." This statement bothered Szilard because "how can anyone know what someone else might invent?" This got him to thinking on the subject.

We must now consider other influences upon Szilard. The previous year, while still in Berlin, he read *The World Set Free*. He later said that it made an impression on him but only as fiction. He did not then try to develop the idea as he had not yet done any work in the area of nuclear physics.

Another important incident of 1932 involves his connection with Otto Mandl, an Austrian timber merchant who lived in London. Mandl had discovered the writings of H. G. Wells and had arranged for them to be published in German. Szilard first met Mandl during his first trip to England in 1929.

In 1932, Mandl moved from London to Berlin. When he met with Szilard again that year, Mandl said that he had thought of a way to save mankind from destruction by a series of wars. He proposed that the efforts of mankind should be focused on an enterprise to leave the earth. Szilard's reaction was that if he wanted to contribute to such an effort, he would go into nuclear physics "because only through the liberation of atomic energy could we obtain the means which would enable man not only to leave the earth but leave the solar system."

Finally, we have the recent discovery of the neutron.

This all came together in Szilard's mind as he took a walk in London sometime after learning of Rutherford's talk. This may have been as early as September 12, 1933 or days or even weeks later; Szilard's versions of this story vary in details.

As he later recalled, he was waiting at a red light at an intersection on Southampton Row. It then occurred to him that:

    . . . if we could find an element which is split by neutrons and which would emit *two* neutrons when it absorbed *one* neutron, such an element, if assembled in sufficiently large mass, could sustain a nuclear chain reaction.

The energy that would be released from the splitting of a single atom (actually the splitting of the nucleus) would be very small. But consider that if one neutron gave rise to two neutrons, then each of those two would give rise to two and so on. Such numbers expand very quickly: 1, 2, 4, 8, 16, 32. After only 20 such doublings, over a million nuclei have been split. As we all know from history, a tremendous amount of energy is released in such a reaction.

The question that we must consider here is how much of Szilard's idea of the chain reaction we can attribute to the influence of *The World Set Free*. Unfortunately, all we can do is speculate.

Which did more to stimulate his interest in nuclear physics: his reading of *The World Set Free* or his conversation with Otto Mandl regarding the salvation of mankind? Or was it their combination?

The various fictional atomic processes mentioned by Wells gave no indication of how they might be accomplished. For that matter, neither did the book by Soddy that Wells used as his primary source. How could they, for the discovery of the particle that was the key to the problem was many years in the future. However, I think that it is interesting to note that the publications by Chadwick regarding the existence of the neutron occurred in the same year that Szilard read *The World Set Free*. Perhaps this established some kind of connection in his mind that only came to the surface when he encountered Rutherford's comments the following year.

Of course, it is possible that there were other influences on Szilard that led him to the idea of the chain reaction not presented here. I feel, however, that we should not disregard *The World Set Free* as being one of the key influences.

What did Szilard do after he came up with the idea for the chain reaction? The most obvious thing was to identify an element, if it existed, that would actually support a chain reaction. So began Szilard's entry into the field of nuclear physics.

His first thought was to try beryllium. He knew that it gave off neutrons when struck by alpha particles. Did this also mean that it would give off extra neutrons when it was struck by neutrons? He tried to stimulate interest in his concept among certain physicists in England but failed to get a favorable response.

The experiments that he was able to perform with beryllium did not, of course, give the result that he expected. He then considered the element indium. One problem was that he was always coming up with new ideas and rarely pursued them to the logical conclusion. One exception was work done in conjunction with Thomas Chalmers. By irradiating an iodine compound, the chemical bond involving the iodine atom would be broken when a new isotope was formed. In general, the Szilard-Chalmers effect provides a means by which a radioactive isotope could be separated from the original compound.

In March 1934, Szilard filed for a British patent on the chain reaction. In the application, he mentioned beryllium, but also mentioned uranium and thorium. To preserve the secrecy of his patent, he assigned it to the British Admiralty in 1936.

The path to the answer to Szilard's search actually began in France. Iréne and Frédéric Joliot-Curie had bombarded aluminum foils with alpha particles. Using a Geiger counter, they could detect the alpha particles. When the alpha source was removed, they continued to get a reading from the aluminum on the Geiger counter. This reading declined in intensity by half after three minutes.

They first suspected that something was wrong with the Geiger counter. When they were told it was working properly, they realized that they had found a way to artificially create radioactive materials. By capturing an alpha particle and then emitting a neutron, an aluminum nucleus is changed to the nucleus of an unstable isotope of phosphorus. This then decayed with a half-life of 3 minutes to a stable isotope of silicon.

It had to be shown that the radioactivity was due to phosphorus. Aluminum foil was exposed to the alpha particles and then dropped into hydrochloric acid. If the Joliot-Curies were correct, the phosphorus should be carried away by the hydrogen gas formed by the reaction. The collected gas was found to be radioactive but the aluminum remaining in solution was not. Another test was used to show that the material carried away with the hydrogen was phosphorus.

The basis of Szilard's idea regarding the chain reaction was that neutrons were easily able to penetrate a nucleus. This also meant that it should be more effective than alpha particles in bombarding other elements to create artificial radioactive isotopes.

The approach using neutrons was vigorously pursued in Rome by Enrico Fermi and his colleagues. After some time, they were able to report that they had induced radioactivity in 20 elements including iron, silicon, phosphorus, chlorine, copper, zinc, magnesium, bromine and lanthanum. Some of the experiments passed the neutrons through materials such as paraffin that contained many hydrogen atoms. Collisions with the hydrogen atoms slowed down the neutrons. Slow neutrons were found to be more effective in creating new isotopes as they were more likely to be captured by the nucleus.

When uranium was bombarded, the results were difficult to interpret. It was first thought that a new element, one step higher on the periodic table, had been created. To understand what was happening, it was necessary to analyze the products that resulted from the uranium bombardment.

The answer to the uranium puzzle was also pursued by scientists other than Fermi. All sorts of theories were proposed to explain what was happening. Most of the efforts concentrated on trying to match the reaction products with elements near uranium, at the top of the periodic table. No one was willing to consider what we know to be true, that the uranium nucleus could be split, thus forming the nuclei of elements much lower in the periodic table.

It was not until December 1938 that Otto Hahn and Fritz Strassmann, after much work to eliminate other possible interpretations, were finally led to the conclusion that one of their reaction products was the element barium. Its atomic number is 56, which places it much lower in the periodic table, far from uranium. When informed of this strange result, Lisa Meitner and her nephew Otto Frisch gave it the proper interpretation.

The search for Szilard's element that could support a chain reaction – a search that was inspired in part by *The World Set Free* – had come to an end.

4

THE RIGHT KIND OF WAVES

The problem was the creation of a type of photograph to be used to display a three-dimensional image. We call this type of photograph a hologram and the process for creating and viewing such images is called holography. There are different types of holograms and though our primary interest will be in one type of hologram and the person who invented it, I will also take a look at two others who were important in the history of holography. We must first look at a Russian scientist who was also a writer of science fiction.

Ivan Antonovich Yefremov (sometimes spelled Efremov) (1908 – 1972) was born in the village of Vyritsa, which is about 45 miles south of St. Petersburg. Some sources say that he was actually born in 1907, others that he was born in 1908 and added a year to his age to appear older as he was growing up. His parents were divorced during the Russian Revolution. His mother married a Red Army commander and left her children with her sister. The sister died of typhus, leaving Yefremov and his siblings on their own.

In the Foreword to a collection of his stories, Yefremov states that he joined a mechanized company of the Sixth Army. Based on his age and the years of the Revolution, Yefremov was just a boy at the time. Was he able to enlist as a regular soldier despite his age, or was he what one source calls a "son of the regiment," which is a term used to denote an orphan adopted by an army unit? His military career, whatever its form, ended after he received a severe concussion from a shell fired, as he claimed, from a British gun-boat.

Yefremov then went to Petrograd. Here a short history of names is required. As founded by Peter the Great, the city was named Saint

Peterburg. In 1914, it was renamed Petrograd. In 1924, it was again renamed, this time to Leningrad. In 1991, following the end of the Soviet Union, the name was returned to St. Peterburg. Note that the Russian version of the name omits the "s", while the English version is St. Petersburg.

When in Petrograd, he took a course in marine navigation and worked as an assistant to a truck driver. During this time, he encountered an article by Petr Petrovich Sushkin. Yefremov identifies him as a paleontologist; his interests also included ornithology, comparative anatomy and the geographical distribution of animals. He contacted Sushkin and was invited to visit him and to explore his museum.

The completion of studies in navigation interrupted his interest in fossils. He sailed as an apprentice seaman in the Far East and on the Caspian Sea. He first entered Leningrad University, but later continued his studies at the Leningrad Mining Institute. At this time, he was alternating winter studies with summer voyages. Yefremov was torn between his interests in the sea and the sciences.

Journeying back to Baku on the Caspian Sea, he briefly had a glimpse of an ancient town that had long ago been submerged. This was the event that turned him towards science. When he arrived at Baku, a telegram came from Sushkin offering him a position at the Academy of Sciences. It was a minor position, that of a technical assistant, but Yefremov accepted.

Yefremov worked in the laboratory during the winter and during the summer looked for fossils all over the Soviet Union. Finishing his university studies, he went on geological expeditions in Siberia and the Far East. He then returned to paleontology. He headed a laboratory that studied the animals of the Paleozoic era. His teacher and mentor Sushkin died in 1928. Yefremov wrote scientific papers but also tried to write stories about his travels, without success. During the Second World War, convalescing after a serious illness, he began to write fiction.

I will not attempt to cover the full range of Yefremov's stories and novels. I will only consider his works that appeared in a collection simply called *Stories*, published in English in 1954 by the Foreign Language Publishing House in Moscow. The collection contains eight stories. Seven of the stories concern expeditions throughout Russia, either for paleontological or geological purposes. The remaining story, "Meeting over the Tuscarora," is about a ship sailing in Far Eastern waters that encounters a shipwreck. Even though Yefremov had abandoned the sea for science, it occasionally crept back into his writings.

The two stories of interest here are the first and last in the collection. The first story is "Shadows of the Past," which was originally published in 1945. A paleontologist named Nikitin heads an expedition into a desert area in Uzbekistan to search for fossils reported by shepherds. A female geologist is assigned to the expedition to survey asphalt deposits. When they arrive in the region, they discover many dinosaur bones. They also discover that the flow of the available water supply is inadequate. The geologist recalls a case where water flow was increased by blasting. They try her suggestion and succeed in obtaining sufficient water.

When they explore the next valley, they come across a large cubical sandstone formation. One face shows a surface described as a "black mirror." The geologist identifies it as asphalt or solidified rosin. The surface is shiny, not weathered and there is sandstone rubble at its base. The conclusion is that the sandstone face collapsed as a result of their blasting a short distance away.

Nikitin delivers a talk on dinosaurs to the members of the expedition in the valley near the sandstone formation. As he is talking, the sunlight hits the rosin surface at a certain angle and they see:

Against the bluish-black slab of fossilized rosin, as from a yawning abyss there appeared a gigantic grey-green ghost. A huge dinosaur was hanging motionless in the air, above the upper edge of a craggy precipice, rearing 30 feet over the heads of the stupefied little group below.

As the sunlight begins to fade, the image also fades and disappears. Nikitin would like to stay and investigate the phenomenon, but conditions dictate that the expedition must depart. Months later, he is still trying to figure out how it was done. He realizes that the very narrow corridor of the valley had acted as the lens of a camera. The real mystery was how the image had been stabilized (fixed) so that it could be seen later. In his research on photography, he comes across a letter from Joseph Niepce to Louis Daguerre.

Some now credit Niepce with being the inventor of photography. He created a print from a photoengraved printing plate in 1825. In 1826 or 1827, he created the oldest surviving photograph, which was the view from a window of his house. The process made use of bitumen, another name for asphalt. This information enables Nikitin to develop a theory that explains how the process occurred naturally to preserve the image of the dinosaur.

Nikitin presents a paper describing what was seen by him and the other members of the expedition. The paper also presents his theory of the natural process that preserved the image. As he has no record of the image, his presentation is criticized. The remainder of the story concerns his attempts to record images in similar asphalt deposits at other locations.

After many unsuccessful attempts, he finally obtains photographic proof. The last scene of the story has him at his desk with a large pile of copies of his article, each containing a color reproduction of the image from the distant past.

The other story of interest from the collection is "Star Ships," which was originally published in 1948. This story is longer than the first and a bit more involved. It begins with the efforts of a paleontologist named Shatrov to recover a notebook of a former student. This student changed his area of interest to astronomy and had developed a theory on the motion of the solar system within the Milky Way Galaxy.

The student, only identified as Victor, had joined the Army during the Second World War. Victor had promised to send a notebook with his theory to Shatrov, but was killed in a great tank battle before he could do so. Following a chance encounter with the Major who had been Victor's commander, he is miraculously able to locate his tank and his student's notebook.

Shatrov then has a meeting with a distinguished astronomer. The only purpose of the meeting seems to be to acquaint the reader with various facts of astronomy.

The story then shifts to a colleague of Shatrov named Davidov, who has been attending a conference of geologists in San Francisco. Davidov is returning by ship across the Pacific Ocean. Here we again see the influence of Yefremov's experience as a seaman. Near one of the Hawaiian Islands, the ship encounters a tsunami, apparently caused by an earthquake in the North Pacific. The ship passes safely through the event, but damage is done to a town on a nearby island. The ship renders assistance to the people of the town and then continues its voyage home. During the voyage, the crew requests an explanation of where the large waves had come from. Davidov delivers a lecture to the crew, again providing information to the reader.

We now have the reunion of Shatrov and Davidov. When they meet, Shatrov reveals a fossil obtained by a Chinese paleontologist who had been killed during the war. The fossil was from Sinkang, by which I assume is meant Xinjiang. This is in the western part of China, bordering Russia, Mongolia, Pakistan and India. The dinosaur fossil fragment shows a small hole that could only have been made while the animal was alive. Another fossil shows a similar hole. The only conclusion possible to the two men is that the holes were made by the weapon of some intelligent creature 70 million years ago.

After concluding that such a creature could not have come from elsewhere in our solar system and that other star systems were too far away, Shatrov presents Victor's theory. His theory was that the solar system follows a path that would have taken it near the center of the Galaxy where the stars are much closer together. This would have occurred 70 million years ago, which corresponds to the age of the fossils. With shorter travel distances, it would have been possible for aliens to have traveled to our solar system and visited Earth.

The problem is in finding a way to verify their theory. They are not able to obtain permission to travel to Xinjiang. The answer comes from a canal project in Alma-Ata, which is in Kazakhstan. A large number of fossils are found in the course of excavating for the canal. Beneath the skull of a dinosaur, a strange smaller skull is found. It is realized that it is the skull of one of the alien visitors. The evidence suggests that when the alien killed the dinosaur he was a bit too close and that its falling body crushed him. Further excavation reveals a number of alien artifacts. One is a disk that on one side appears to show a transparent surface under the grime. When the surface is cleaned:

The two scientists involuntarily recoiled. From the deep bottom of the absolutely transparent layer, magnified by some mysterious optical device to its natural proportions, there looked out at them a strange but an undoubtedly human face. Its dominating feature were its huge prominent eyes, which looked straight ahead. They were like pools reflecting the eternal mystery of creation, glowing with intelligence and an intense will, like two powerful rays directed through the brittle wall of glass into the boundless vistas of universal space. In those eyes there burned the light of the boundless courage of reason, unabashed by the awareness of the ruthless laws of the universe, reveling in the agonies and joys of knowledge.

The story concludes with the realization that meetings would eventually occur with the inhabitants of other worlds. This meant that the task was to first unite the peoples of our world and then proceed to the unification of worlds.

For the moment, I will just note that both of these stories involve strange means of reproducing images. We will now leave Ivan Yefremov and his stories and look at the man who received the Nobel Prize for the invention of holography.

Dennis Gabor (1900 – 1979) was born in Budapest, Hungary. His name at birth was actually Günszberg Dénes. In 1902, the family changed their name from Günszberg to Gabor, in the same manner as the family of Leo Szilard. Dennis had two younger brothers, George and André. Their father was the director of a large industrial enterprise and the boys were raised in a cultured environment. They learned English, French and German from their governesses.

Because of tutoring and his extensive reading, Dennis claimed that he was ahead of the curriculum in school and knew more than his teachers in subjects such as physics. He made an early decision to be an engineer. This pleased his father who had been unable to pursue his own desire to become an engineer due to family financial problems when he was in his teens. The father did everything he could to support the scientific and technical interests of his sons.

Although he took the examination required for admission to the University, Dennis was also facing military service in World War I. In the spring of 1918, he entered officer training in Lugos, Romania. In the fall of 1918, he began the last part of his training in northern Italy. The war ended with him never having been in combat. He then entered Budapest Technical University to major in mechanical engineering. In his third year at the University, he received an order to register for military service. As a consequence of this order, he left Hungary to study electrical engineering at the Technische Hochschule in Berlin.

Gabor was not pleased with the situation at that school. He said:

> There were far too many students and there was hardly any personal contact between students and teachers. It was a sort of slot machine into which one had to throw no end of machine designs, essays and papers and out came a diploma (1924) in the end.

One thing that he did enjoy was attending the Physical Colloquium at Friedrich Wilhelm University. He also attended Einstein's seminar on statistical mechanics that had been arranged by fellow Hungarian Leo Szilard. After receiving his Diploma, Gabor remained at the Technische Hochschule to obtain his Dr. Ing.

Gabor's advisor for his thesis research was unable to suggest a suitable problem to pursue. The problem that he found involved electrical transients, which are extremely fast changes that may occur in circuits. One example of a transient is a voltage spike induced on the power line by a lightning strike. Gabor developed a means of capturing image of transients using an oscilloscope. Such equipment was still in a primitive state during the 1920s. In his design, the photographic plate was placed inside the tube used to display the waveform to increase its sensitivity. He also designed a circuit that kept the electron beam diverted from the plate until the transient arrived.

After he received his degree, Gabor went to work for the firm of Siemens and Halske. When his contract was not renewed in 1933, following the Nazis coming to power, he returned to Hungary. In 1934, he went to England, having obtained a job offer from the British Thompson Houston Company. Once he was in England, he found out that the people were very friendly. Referring to letters from Dennis, his brother André said:

> he had already made a number of friends, had been the guest of several families, and that he had only just realized how unfriendly the Germans were: after 12 years in their country Dennis had made fewer friends than in England after a few weeks.

Gabor would remain at British Thompson Houston until 1948. One feature of his employment there was that Marjorie Butler also worked there; she became his wife in August 1936.

I am not going to attempt to describe the range of problems on which Gabor worked from 1934 to 1948. I will consider only the area of electron optics. In the same manner that a physical lens will affect the path of a beam of light, either magnetic or electric fields may be used to affect the path of charged particles such as electrons.

It was shown that the magnetic field created by the same type of coil that Gabor had used in his oscilloscope acted upon an electron beam in the same manner that a convex lens acts upon a beam of light. This meant that it was possible to obtain magnification. In 1931, Max Knoll and Ernst Ruska demonstrated the first electron microscope. This was done at the Technische Hochschule in Berlin where Gabor had obtained his degrees. One of the components of the microscope was a modification of the coil from his oscilloscope.

Gabor had earlier speculated on the possibility of an electron microscope but did not pursue it at the time. The paper describing the focusing effects of the magnetic field appeared only after he had left the Hochschule for Siemens and Halske. Perhaps disappointed at not making these discoveries himself, from that point on he pursued his interests in electron optics.

To understand the advantage of an electron microscope, we must consider the electron wavelength. It might seem strange to speak of the wavelength of a particle. We have no trouble of speaking of light waves even though we know that light exists as photons. The wavelength of an electron depends on its momentum, which means it depends on its velocity. The wavelength of an electron can be several orders of magnitude shorter than photons of visible light. This means that an electron microscope can have higher magnification and be capable of resolving smaller objects than a light microscope.

Before proceeding any further, it is necessary to discuss a number of concepts so that the work of Gabor and others may be understood. A sinusoidal waveform may be described in terms of its amplitude A, frequency ω and phase ϕ according to the formula

$$f(t) = A \sin (\omega t + \phi)$$

The amplitude A is the magnitude of its maximum positive or negative values. The frequency ω tells us how quickly the waveform repeats per second of time t. If the phase ϕ is some value other than zero, it means that the waveform has the same shape and amplitude but is shifted in time.

Light waves, like any electromagnetic waves, may be described in terms of their amplitude and phase. When a conventional photograph is taken, each point on the film (or detector) records only the intensity of the light focused upon it by the lens. Intensity is determined only by the amplitude; any phase information is lost.

When making a hologram of an object, there is a reference light beam and the beam that consists of the light scattered from the object. If you add two waveforms, interference is the name given to the result. For example, consider the intersection of the ripples from two pebbles tossed into a pond. It is the extremely complex interference pattern resulting from the two beams that is recorded by the film when making a hologram. This interference pattern depends on the phase of the light waves within the beams as well as their amplitude. To view the hologram, a reference beam is applied to the recorded interference pattern. This results in a duplication of the original beam scattered from the object, with both its amplitude and phase information restored.

Two waves are coherent if they have a constant relative phase. Temporal coherence measures how a waveform interferes with a version of itself delayed by time τ. The coherence time τ_c is the delay over which the amplitude or phase has varied such that the interference is affected. If a waveform is of a single frequency, the coherence time is infinite; the result is always the same no matter how much you shift it in time. Coherence length is τ_c multiplied by the speed of light. Spatial coherence measures the ability of a wave to interfere at two points in space.

Holography requires a source of light that is both spatially and temporally coherent. White light sources such as light bulbs are considered incoherent. The usual source of coherent light is from lasers. Depending on the type of laser, the coherence length can range from tens of centimeters up to kilometers.

Now let us return to Dennis Gabor and the electron microscope.

In 1947, Gabor was considering how to increase the resolving power of the electron microscope. His solution is best described by quoting from his Nobel Prize lecture:

> Why not take a bad electron picture, but one which contains the *whole* information, and correct it by optical means? It was clear to me for some time that this could be done, if at all, only with coherent electron beams, with electron waves which have a definite phase. But an ordinary photograph loses the phase completely, it records only the intensities. No wonder we lose the phase, if there is nothing to compare it with! Let us see what happens if we add a standard to it, a "coherent background". . . . The interference of the object wave and of the coherent background or "reference wave" will then produce interference fringes. There will be maxima wherever the phases of the two waves were identical. Let us make a hard positive record, so that it transmits only at the maxima, and illuminate it with the reference source alone. Now the phases are of course right for the reference source A, but as at the slits the phases are identical, they must be right also for B; therefore the wave of B must also appear, *reconstructed.*

This arrangement may be seen in Figure 2. Aside from the fact that he was proposing the use of coherent electron beams instead of a coherent light source, the process is the same as in conventional holography. He also found that a positive of the image was not necessary; a negative would do as well.

In the experiments that he performed, Gabor was not able to make use of lasers, for their invention would not occur for many years. By using a high-pressure mercury lamp and filtering its output he was able to obtain monochromatic light. Such a source, however, has a coherence length of 0.1 mm. This meant that he had to work with very small objects and very small images. The results that he obtained, however, were sufficient to demonstrate that the principle was correct. Some additional work was done by Gabor and others and papers were published. Nothing really happened until the development of lasers provided suitable coherent sources.

One important limitation of Gabor's in-line approach is that two images are created when the hologram is viewed. One image is in the position of the original object and the other is on the other side of the

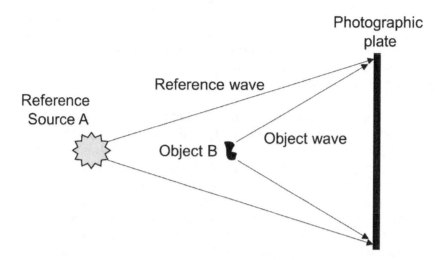

Figure 2. Gabor's method for creating a hologram.

hologram. It is impossible to separate the images by optical means and this limited the usefulness of the reconstructed image.

We will now consider the work done in holography that was inspired by one of the stories of Ivan Yefremov.

Yuri Nikolaievich Denisyuk (1927 – 2006) was born in Sochi to Nikolai Nestorovich and Elena Konstantinovna Denisyuk. Most of you should have heard of Sochi as it was the host city for the XXII Olympic Winter Games and XI Paralympic Winter Games, both in 2014. Most recently, it was a host city for the 2018 FIFA World Cup.

Yuri's father was a driver and his mother worked in the restaurant where her mother Natalia Dmitrievna Sizmina was a chef. Following the birth of Yuri, things were good for several years. Or as good as they could be in the Soviet Union under Josef Stalin. Then Yuri's father, Nikolai, was labeled an "enemy of the people" and sent to a labor camp. The exact charges against him are not known. Elena divorced Nikolai to save herself and the family from the fate of her husband. Nikolai was released from the camp in the 1950s but did not reunite with his family.

Elena now pursued her dream of becoming an engineer. She became a student at the Leningrad Polytechnic Institute, which is now known as Peter the Great St. Petersburg Polytechnic University. Yuri stayed behind in Sochi with his grandmother Natalia. A few years later, both Yuri and his grandmother came to Leningrad to be with Elena. The year of this move is not known, so it may have occurred while she was still a student.

Following graduation, Elena began working as an engineer at a factory in Leningrad. Possibly more important, she found a new husband. Elena's second husband was Solomon Solomonovich Granat. He had graduated from St. Petersburg University. Solomon was well educated and knew French, English, German and Greek. He travelled as a specialist in the pulp and paper industry and was involved in the design of large machines for paper production.

Their residence in Leningrad was at No. 23 on 6th Red Army Street. It was a communal apartment with five rooms for 12 tenants. There was only one toilet for all of the tenants. Only cold water and no gas for the stoves; one of Yuri's jobs was to bring in the firewood.

Yuri appears to have gotten on very well with his stepfather. Because of Solomon's technical background, he was probably a very important source of Yuri's interests in science and technology. There were other influences on Yuri. He read science fiction, but his favorite authors are not known. Yuri was also a reader of the Russian popular science magazine *Nature* (Priroda) which first appeared in January 1912.

Now we come to World War II. The German invasion of the Soviet Union began on June 22, 1941. Solomon and his brother went to the front; Solomon survived the war, his brother did not. Leningrad had been bombed very early in the invasion. For their protection, many children such as Yuri had been sent to rural villages. Yuri was in the village of Verevkino in the Novgorod oblast. But the grandmother was afraid the family would be separated. As the German forces were getting closer, she convinced Elena to go to Verevkino by rail and bring Yuri back to Leningrad. The next day the rail line was bombed. When the village was taken, the children still there were sent to Germany. A good sign that even mothers should pay attention to their mother's suggestions.

The last road to the city of Leningrad was taken by the Germans on September 8, 1941. The siege lasted until January 27, 1944. Although there were casualties due to artillery fire and air raids during the course of the siege, the greatest number of deaths were by starvation. This caused the deaths of 1,500,000 soldiers and civilians. Another 1,400,000 civilians were evacuated. In the spring of 1942, Yuri's family was evacuated to Kolomna in the Moscow oblast.

Kolomna is located about 100 km southeast of Moscow. While in Kolomna, Yuri completed his secondary education. He then entered a tekhnikum that dealt with shipbuilding. A tekhnikum was part of the Soviet system of specialized secondary education, a level above the ordinary vocational schools. A graduate of a tekhnikum could apply to an institution of higher education; a graduate of a vocational school could not.

In June 1944, five months after the siege of Leningrad had ended, Yuri and his mother returned to that city. He continued his studies, now at the Leningrad Shipbuilding Tekhnikum, graduating in 1947. Although he began doing design work at a shipbuilding facility in Leningrad, Yuri knew that this was not the career he wanted; he wanted to be a physicist.

He began his studies at the Leningrad Institute of Fine Mechanics and Optics (LIFMO) The acronym in Russian is ЛИТМО. Like many institutions in the former Soviet Union, it has undergone many name changes. It is now known as ITMO University. Yuri began by taking evening courses. He soon realized that this was not the way to get to the career he envisioned for himself. He was then able to gain entry to the normal daytime course of study in the Department of Physical Engineering, beginning in 1948.

In 1952, Yuri married classmate Galina Vasilyevna Kremez. In 1954, Yuri graduated from LIFMO. He had focused on spectroscopy and the title of his final thesis was "Features of the Spark Discharge." He received a "red diploma," signifying that he received high grades and excellent marks on his thesis.

When the assignments were made after graduation, Yuri expected that he would be sent to the State Optical Institute (ГОИ) in Leningrad. He was assigned instead to the Krasnogorsk Mechanical Plant in the Moscow oblast, which had been established in 1942 to provide optical systems to the military. Following the war, it also began producing consumer products such as lenses and cameras. One problem with Yuri's assignment was that there were no apartments for couples. By going to the Ministry in Moscow, he succeeded in getting his assignment changed to the State Optical Institute.

The State Optical Institute was founded in 1918. It engages in both basic and applied research in optical problems. As one might expect, a large amount of its work was in support of the Soviet armed forces. When Yuri began working there in 1954, approximately 800 people were at the Institute.

Yuri was placed in the group that developed optical instruments for the Soviet Navy. He later described it as "very dull work relating to the development of conventional optical devices consisting of lenses and prisms." There was occasionally some excitement. One project was to develop optical systems to aid in the launching of ballistic missiles from submarines. Part of Yuri's job was to test the systems on submarines in both the Baltic and Black Sea Fleets. During one test voyage, the submarine had some difficulty in surfacing, but fortunately for Yuri it was able to resolve the problem.

There is no doubt that Denisyuk was inspired by one of Yefremov's stories. Yefremov claimed that it was from "Shadows from the Past." To counter that, we have a direct statement from Denisyuk. In his paper "My Way in Holography," he referred to his work at the State Optical Institute in Leningrad. He said:

At the time, I was very fond of reading science-fiction stories. Among them, I came across the story "Star Ships" by the well known soviet writer Yu. Efremov. One of the episodes from this story greatly impressed me. In this episode, contemporary archaeologists, while excavating a site where reasonable creatures from a foreign planet had been hunting for dinosaurs millions of years ago, accidentally found a strange plate.

Even though we have a definite statement from Denisyuk with regard to the identity of the story, there remains a small mystery. As quoted from the same article, the description of the discovery of the plate was presented by Denisyuk as:

A thrill pierced the hearts of both professors when the dust had been removed from the surface of the plate. From a deep, absolutely transparent layer, a strange face was looking at them. The face was enlarged by some unknown optical method to its natural size and was three dimensional in its shape. The most striking feature of this face was its unbelievable animation, especially in its eyes.

The corresponding description as taken from the English version of "Star Ships" in *Stories* is:

The two scientists involuntarily recoiled. From the deep bottom of the absolutely transparent layer, magnified by some mysterious optical device to its natural proportions, there looked out at them a strange but an undoubtedly human face. Its dominating features were its huge prominent eyes, which looked straight ahead.

It should be noted that the Denisyuk version specifically refers to the three-dimensional nature of the image. If we look instead at the quote taken from *Stories* plus all material that follows it, there is no mention at all of a three-dimensional image. Is the difference simply due to Denisyuk's erroneous recollection of what he had read?

Denisyuk then wondered if it would be possible to create images such a portrayed in the story using modern optics. Obviously, the story provided no hint of any kind as to how this might be accomplished.

According to Denisyuk, the starting point of his work was easy. Although he was not aware of the work of Gabor, he began from the same basis. If one could somehow record what he called the "wave field" of light scattered from an object, it would be possible to later reproduce that wave field. This would recreate the appearance of the original object since the wave field would include the necessary phase information. Some descriptions of holography make use of the term "light field" in the same sense as Denisyuk's term.

I will begin by showing how a Denisyuk hologram is created and viewed. I will then describe the many difficulties that he encountered in arriving at that result. The important thing to note is that unlike Gabor's approach where the reference beam and object beam are in the same direction, Denisyuk's approach has the two beams coming from opposite directions. The following figures and the corresponding explanation are based on an article by Denisyuk.

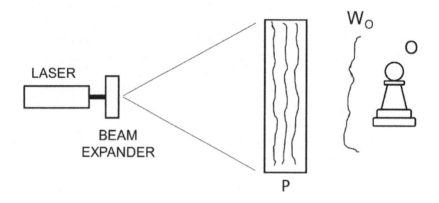

Figure 3. Creating a Denisyuk hologram.

In Figure 3, we have a laser and a beam expander, a photographic plate P and an arbitrary object O. P is a photographic plate which is sufficiently transparent to permit some of the incident laser light to pass through to illuminate O. The incident light wave interferes with the object wave W_O that is composed of light scattered from object O. The interference creates what is known as a standing wave pattern. The lines inside the photographic plate represent the points on the standing wave where the intensity is the greatest. Obviously, there would be more than three such lines in the physical case. When the film is developed, each of the lines forms a reflective surface within the volume of P.

What has to be done to view a Denisyuk hologram? This is shown in Figure 4.

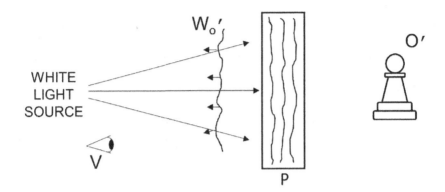

Figure 4. Viewing a Denisyuk hologram.

To reconstruct the image, we may make use of a white light source. When this light strikes the developed plate P, light is reflected back from each of the internal surfaces. These reflections combine to form the object wave W_O'. The various reflective surfaces select out only the frequency of the laser light that was used to create the image. Therefore, a viewer V will see a monochrome image O' that is indistinguishable from the original object O.

Presented this way, it all seems so simple and obvious, doesn't it? But as Denisyuk found out, actually getting there was not quite so simple. His original thought was to record the interference pattern on the surface of the film. This would have required a photographic emulsion thinner than for any films that were available. Such a problem could have ended his research then and there.

The solution to his problem came from the work of Gabriel Lippmann (1845 – 1921) who was born in Luxembourg. His family moved to France in 1848. He was sent by the French government to Germany, where he received a Ph.D. from Heidelberg University in 1873. Lippmann became a professor at the Sorbonne in 1878.

Lippmann developed a process for creating color photographs without making use of dyes or pigments. His process made use of a thin photographic emulsion which contained extremely small grains of silver halide. A silver halide is a compound of silver with a halogen such as bromine, chlorine or iodine. Silver halides are sensitive to light. A temporary mirror of liquid mercury is placed at the rear of the emulsion. The picture is taken in sunlight and requires long exposure times. The light that passes through is reflected by the mirror and interferes with the incident light to create standing waves that are preserved within the volume of the emulsion.

For the purpose of viewing, the developed plate is backed with a black anti-reflection coating. The plate is illuminated with white light. Light of the wavelength that created a particular layer within the emulsion is reflected back to the viewer. This causes the image to be displayed in its original colors. Although the process was clearly successful in creating color images, it could not be developed commercially. Aside from the required long exposures, there was no way to create color prints on paper. For his invention of the method of color photography based on the interference phenomenon, Gabriel Lippmann received the Nobel Prize in Physics in 1908.

Denisyuk realized that Lippmann's approach, recording the patterns within the volume of the emulsion, was the solution. He was, however, faced with additional problems. Lippmann had used bright sunlight for his exposures. Denisyuk needed to use a monochromatic light source. Like Gabor, he used a high-pressure mercury lamp, selecting a particular wavelength by means of a filter. With such a dim source, he needed photographic plates much more sensitive than those used by Lippmann. With the assistance of Dr. Rebekka Protas at the State Optical Institute, he was able to increase the sensitivity of Lippmann plates a thousand times and more.

The use of the mercury lamp also meant that the coherence length was only several tenths of a millimeter. This limited the depth of relief of the object to be photographed. Denisyuk has stated that he regrets not choosing the relief of the face of a coin. What he did choose were convex mirrors that were very shallow. The proof of his concept was that the resulting image acted like a convex mirror. If a beam of parallel light rays from the mercury source was directed at his "wave photograph," it produced a divergent light beam.

Denisyuk's work, performed at the State Optical Institute, was meant to be the research for his *kandidat* degree. This is the Russian equivalent of a doctoral level scientific degree and is translated into other languages as a Doctor of Philosophy (Ph. D.). He had been supported by his superior at the Institute, but had performed his research without supervision as the person suggested as his supervisor had died.

It was only as he was working on his dissertation that Denisyuk became aware of the work that had been done by Gabor. It was necessary to make changes to articles in preparation to include references to Gabor.

The publication of articles describing the research is a necessary condition to obtain the *kandidat* degree. He had trouble getting the recommendation necessary for publication as he found that he had enemies. He was finally able to obtain support from one academician at the Institute, Vladimir Linnik, who presented his paper to the Academy of Sciences.

It would be nice to say that Denisyuk met with instant acclaim when his result became known. But this was not the case. As with Gabor, his research had been done before lasers became available. The need to make use of a mercury lamp limited what could be accomplished other than a demonstration of the concept. It was perhaps for this limitation that he was not granted the *kandidat* degree until 1964. The importance of Denisyuk's work was recognized in the Soviet Union only when lasers became available and work on holography was done in other countries, most particularly the United States. In 1970, he received the Lenin Prize, the first of many awards at home and abroad.

So far, we have seen how Gabor and Denisyuk came to their approaches to holography. There is one more bit of holographic history that must be related. One other man made it possible for the hologram to transition from a laboratory curiosity limited in its scope and capability to a means of creating images of objects that amazed the world.

Emmett Leith (1927 – 2005) was born in Detroit, Michigan. He served in the Navy at the end of World War II, but saw no action. He attended college at Wayne State University in Detroit. Leith majored in physics, receiving his Bachelor of Science in 1949 and his Master's degree in 1952.

He went to work at the Willow Run Laboratory in Ann Arbor, which was run by the University of Michigan. One problem being studied at Willow Run concerned radar. The objective was to develop a radar system that would be capable of creating images of high resolution. To obtain the desired resolution with a conventional radar would have required an antenna too large for an airplane.

The solution was in what became known as Synthetic Aperture Radar (SAR). Consider a plane flying in a straight line. A radar antenna points from the side of the aircraft and is angled down toward the ground. As the plane flies along, it takes a series of radar images. By the proper processing of these images (the details of which I will not go into here) the system obtains a result that synthesizes the performance of an antenna much longer than the real antenna. There are many books available to explain SAR, one of which is *Introduction to Airborne Radar* by George W. Stimson.

The difficulty was in the amount of processing that was required. Today we are used to very high-speed computers with a lot of processing power. Such computers simply did not exist at that time. The solution was in optical processing. Leith was in a position to make a contribution to the project. He had taken a number of undergraduate optics courses, which gave him an advantage over the electrical engineers on the project.

If the data to be processed can be expressed as an image or a signal, it can be fed into a combination of lenses, transparencies, filters and other optical elements. These can perform addition, multiplication and more complex mathematical processes. Such a system can be designed to be either incoherent or coherent. Certain of the mathematical operations are much easier to realize with a coherent system. The only source of suitable light available at the time was, as in the other cases that I have presented, from a filtered mercury lamp.

The radar data was recorded on photographic film in two dimensions on the basis of azimuth (parallel to flight path) and range (perpendicular to flight path). Like a hologram, simply looking at such a record shows no useful pattern. As an intermediate step in the processing, however, the film is illuminated by coherent light. Based on his observations of the results of this step, Leith was able to develop a theory based on physical optics that would lead him to holography. He later remarked that if computers of sufficient power had existed at the time, the connection to holography might not have been realized.

Although the development of SAR was a success, the secrecy of the project prevented Leith from making his developments in optical processing public. By this time, he had become aware of Gabor's work and saw that it was related to the processing work he had been doing. Working with a colleague, Juris Upatnieks, Leith found a way to separate the two images generated by a hologram.

In their holography work, Leith and Upatnieks made use of the same source as their SAR work; a filtered mercury lamp. The availability of lasers did not instantly solve their problems, but by the spring of 1963 they had achieved excellent results in what they called "lensless photography." Their work was presented at the spring 1964 meeting of the Optical Society of America and included a demonstration of hologram of a brass model of a locomotive. A description of the event says that:

> A line of optical scientists and engineers wound down the hallways of the hotel as they patiently waited to see the 3D images that were absolutely unprecedented in their realism and accuracy.

Such results were possible through their development of what is known as "off-axis" holography.

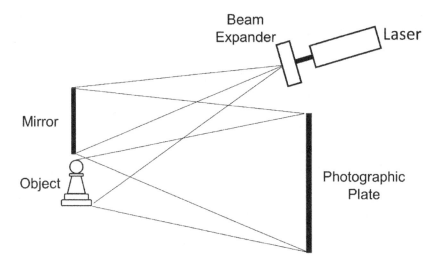

Figure 5. Creating an Off-Axis hologram.

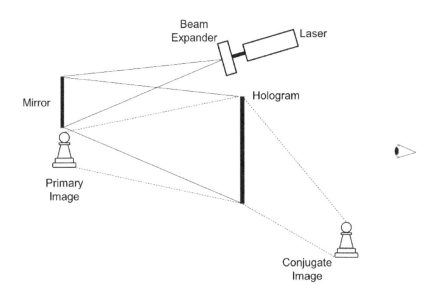

Figure 6. Viewing an Off-Axis hologram.

The basic process is illustrated in Figure 5. The coherent light beam, which is obtained from a laser, is first passed through a beam expander. Part of the beam strikes a mirror and is directed to the photographic plate and forms the reference beam. The other part of the beam illuminates the object. The light scattered from the object to the photographic plate forms the object beam. There are many possible arrangements that may be used to obtain the two beams. Some arrangements employ a beam splitter, in which part of the light is passed through and part is reflected at an angle. The object beam interferes with the reference beam and the photographic plate records the interference pattern.

This is exactly how Gabor's approach is used to create a hologram, as far as the creation and recording of the interference pattern is concerned. The difference lies with how the beams are oriented with regard to the photographic plate. As shown in Figure 5, the object beam is in-line with the plate, but the reference beam strikes the plate at an angle. This difference is critically important when the resulting hologram is viewed. When the laser is used to recreate the image, the observer to the right sees the image of the object in its original in-line position, as shown in Figure 6. The second image, instead of being in-line as in Gabor's approach, is now shifted to one side by twice the angle of the reference beam and no longer interferes with the first image. Another important advantage of this technique is that the viewer is not looking directly into the laser beam.

Leith became an associate professor at the University of Michigan in 1965 and a full professor in 1968. Although a professor, he still only possessed a M.S. in Physics. This detail was finally taken care of in 1978 when he received his Ph.D. in electrical engineering from Wayne State University.

In this chapter, I have presented the stories of three men who created the field of holography. Their stories show the different sources of inspiration that an inventor may encounter. Gabor was inspired by trying to solve problems in Electron Microscopy and Leith by the optical processing used in Synthetic Aperture Radar. But in the case of the third man, Yuri Denisyuk, we have proof by his own words that he was inspired to develop his form of holography by reading a work of science fiction.

5

TAMING THE SERPENT

The problem was oil. To be precise, it was a shortage of oil.

In 1955, Britain imported 39.8 million tons of oil from the Middle East. At 7.4 barrels to the ton (the exact value depends on the specific gravity of the oil), we would be looking at 294.5 million barrels of oil. At 42 gallons to the barrel, that works out to 12.4 billion gallons. The point I am trying to make is that whether we speak of tons, barrels or gallons, that is a **lot** of oil. And of that quantity, 23.3 million tons or about 59% of the total was transported by tankers that transited the Suez Canal. The rest was transported by tankers loading from pipelines that terminated in eastern Mediterranean ports.

Then in 1956, there occurred the Suez Crisis. A series of events led Egypt to nationalize the Canal on July 26. Although attempts were made to resolve the problem diplomatically, an agreement was reached between Britain, France and Israel to take military action. Such actions by Israel began on October 26, followed by the British and the French on October 31. Part of the response of Egypt was to sink or disable more than 40 ships present in the Canal, which closed it to all shipping. A cease fire took place on November 6 and the troops were soon withdrawn from Egyptian territory. An important result of the Crisis was that the Canal was blocked to all shipping until April 24, 1957.

If you were a tanker captain in late 1956 and early 1957, you were then looking at much longer voyages than normal. In going from the Arabian Gulf to England through the Suez Canal, the length of the trip is about 6,400 nautical miles (11,853 km). But with the Canal blocked, the trip would have to be made around the Cape of Good Hope. This is a voyage of 11,300 nautical miles (20,928 km), an increase of 76% over the Canal route.

The oil sources in the Middle East still existed, and Britain still had its tanker fleet. What was the problem? With the same number of tankers requiring much longer times to deliver their oil, less oil was being delivered. Or to look at it another way, any tanker using the longer route could make less round trips in a given period of time. Britain would have to find more tankers to make deliveries from the Middle East. It was possible for Britain to get oil from other sources such as the United States, but then additional tankers would also be needed to transport that oil. Britain was looking at a tanker shortage and the rationing of oil and gasoline.

One potential solution came from a man whose interests included conjuring, flames, and science fiction.

William Rede Hawthorne (1913 – 2011) was born in Benton, Newcastle upon Tyne. His education began at Dragon School in Oxford and continued at Westminster School in London. At Westminster, he won an exhibition (scholarship) to Trinity College, Cambridge University.

Starting at Cambridge in 1931, his first area of study was in mathematics, but he then switched to mechanical engineering with a particular interest in thermodynamics. His other interests at Trinity included rowing (which could be called typical) and conjuring (which is probably not so typical). His interest in conjuring led to him joining the Pentacle Club, a connection he maintained throughout his life.

Thermodynamics grew from the efforts to understand the operation of early steam engines and to improve their efficiencies. A proper understanding of concepts such as temperature, heat, energy and work and their relationships led to the development of the laws of thermodynamics, which may be applied to any system in which there is a transfer of energy.

Hawthorne graduated with a B.A. in 1934, receiving a prize honoring the greatest distinction in thermodynamics in a section of the Tripos (undergraduate examinations) as well as sharing another prize for the best performance in the examinations.

Following graduation, Hawthorne went to work as a graduate apprentice at Babcock & Wilcox, Ltd. in Renfrew, Scotland. The parent American firm Babcock & Wilcox had been founded in 1867 in Providence, Rhode Island. The boilers that they manufactured and sold were based on the water-tube boiler invented and patented by Steven Wilcox. The British company was formed in 1891 and the manufacturing facility at Renfrew established in 1895.

In 1935, Hawthorne won a Commonwealth Fund Fellowship to study chemical engineering at the Massachusetts Institute of Technology. Working with Professor H. C. Hottel, he did research on the dynamics of chemical combustion – what happens when you burn something in air. The general assumption at the time was that a gaseous fuel would burn completely if enough oxygen was available. Hawthorne's research showed that in fires that burned quickly, there were eddies of unburned gaseous fuel. An eddy is the swirl that occurs in a flowing liquid or a gas when that flow is turbulent. He also showed that there was a relationship between the amount of turbulence and the flame length. The title of his thesis was "The Mixing of Gas and Air in Flames."

Hawthorne returned to Babcock & Wilcox to work as a development engineer. He briefly returned to Cambridge, Massachusetts in April 1939 for two reasons. The first was to receive his Sc.D. degree from MIT. The second was to marry Barbara Runkle, who was a granddaughter of John D. Runkle, the second president of MIT. So now there was a second connection between Hawthorne and MIT.

He continued to work at Babcock & Wilcox until the outbreak of World War II. In 1940 he became a scientific officer in the Ministry of Aircraft Production and was posted to the Royal Aircraft Establishment at Farnborough. We now come to his most important contribution to the war effort. There were two parallel efforts to develop a jet engine in the years leading up to World War II. One was by Hans Joachim Ohain in Nazi Germany. The other was in Britain by Frank Whittle. To understand Hawthorne's contributions to the development of the jet engine, we must now take a brief look at Whittle.

Frank Whittle (1907 – 1996) was born in Earlsdon, a suburb of Coventry. As he was growing up, he wished to be a pilot. His obvious path was to join the Royal Air Force. At the age of 15, after several attempts, he was accepted for the RAF Mechanics Apprentice School. By the time he had completed his training at the school, his demonstrated abilities led to a recommendation for officer training at the RAF College. Following his graduation from the RAF College in 1928, he was commissioned as a Pilot Officer. He then served at a series of postings and gradually rose through the ranks.

At one point in his RAF career, it became necessary for Whittle to specialize in either signals, armament, navigation or engineering. He selected engineering and was then posted to attend the Officers' Engineering Course in August 1932. He scored a composite score of 98 on the entrance exams and then went on to complete the 24-month course in 18 months. His exceptional performance in the Officers' Engineering Course led to him being sent to Cambridge University for two years of study. By 1938, he had been promoted to Squadron Leader.

Let us return to his time at the RAF College. A necessary requirement for graduation was the writing of a thesis. The subject of Whittle's thesis was "Future Developments in Aircraft Design." Whittle spoke of the possibility of aircraft flying at speeds greater than possible at that time. Unfortunately, he did not suggest the possibility of using the type of engine that he eventually developed – the turbojet.

A turbojet engine in its simplest form consists of (1) an air intake, (2) a compressor, (3) a combustion chamber, (4) a turbine and (5) an exhaust nozzle. The air enters through the intake and passes to the compressor which increases its temperature and pressure. The compressed air is then mixed with fuel in the combustion chamber or chambers. The hot gases resulting from the burning of the fuel pass through the turbine on the way to the exhaust nozzle. The turbine is connected with the compressor by a shaft, so the rotation of the turbine drives the compressor. The hot gases exit through the exhaust nozzle and provide the thrust to propel the aircraft.

Starting in 1929, Whittle began working on the idea of a turbojet engine. It would take quite a bit of space here to give a detailed discussion of the many difficulties that he encountered. Such a discussion would divert us from the path of this chapter. There are many articles and books that may be examined to learn the story of Whittle and the turbojet. One such article will be encountered in a few paragraphs. A useful book is *The Jet Race and the Second World War* by Sterling Pavelec, which looks at the development of jets in Germany, England and the United States. There were a wide range of technical problems that Whittle and his team had to solve. Although he was permitted to continue his work on the development of the turbojet while serving as an RAF officer, there were at times a problem of lack of official support as well as a chronic shortage of funds.

One of the most difficult problems in the quest to develop the turbojet was that of combustion. An early version of supplying the fuel was based on the principle of the Primus kerosene stove. In this design, the fuel is passed through tubes that are heated by the flame. It is vaporized fuel that is injected into the burner. This approach did not produce the level of combustion that was expected. One of the keys to the solution of the combustion problem was the replacement of vaporized fuel by liquid fuel injection. This was accomplished by the Lubbock burner, developed by Isaac Lubbock of the Shell Petroleum Company, which introduced the fuel in a mist of droplets rather than as a vapor.

A number of descriptions of the development of the turbojet by Whittle, such as the book by Pavelec, only mention the contribution of Lubbock. There is no mention at all of Hawthorne. Other sources state that Hawthorne was loaned from the Royal Aircraft Establishment at Farnborough in 1940 to help Whittle solve his combustion problems but give no details of what he did. Given his thesis research on combustion and his practical experience at Babcock & Wilcox, Hawthorne would appear to have been the ideal person to be directed to the problem. It became necessary to locate a source that gave more details about the solution of the problem.

The answer came in a paper "The Early History of the Aircraft Gas Turbine in Britain" that was published in 1991. The author of this paper was none other than William Hawthorne! He described the wide range of technical problems that had to be solved in areas such as the compressor and turbine, finally arriving at the difficulties of combustion. It seems that the best approach here is simply to quote from the paper:

> With several others, I was sent on loan from the RAE to lead a group on combustion at Power Jets. At this time, I. Lubbock of Shell had developed a variable geometry swirl-type atomizer around which he built a combustion chamber somewhat similar in design to a domestic oil burner. . . The Lubbock fuel nozzle . . . gave good results, but a good fuel injector is not the only requirement for good combustion. I had done my thesis on laminar and turbulent diffusion flames and knew the importance of aerodynamics in the combustion process. It surprised me that others did not see that as much care was required in characterizing the aerodynamic features of a combustion chamber as in the design of a blade for a compressor or turbine. It was several months before an adequate flow pattern was obtained which gave good combustion and stability over a wide range without carbon deposits, and a uniform gas temperature distribution at inlet to the turbine nozzles.

So now we have at least a general idea of Hawthorne's contributions to the turbojet. There were additional problems with the engine to be solved, but the Whittle W.1 engine, mounted in an aircraft called the Gloster E.28/39, made its official first flight on May 15, 1941. It should be noted that the first flight of any aircraft with a jet engine took place in Germany on August 27, 1939.

Following his work with Whittle, Hawthorne returned to the Royal Aircraft Establishment. He served as head of the Gas Turbine Division, another choice that seems logical given his knowledge and experience in the area. In 1944, he was briefly sent to the United States to transfer information regarding the development of jet engines. For the remainder of the war and shortly thereafter, he was in the Ministry of Supply.

Then it was back to research, and back to MIT. In 1946, he returned there as an associate professor of mechanical engineering. He became George Westinghouse Professor of Mechanical Engineering in 1948. Some of this work was done in conjunction with Professor Hottel who had continued to do research in the area of flames. This led to the development of what they called *unmixedness* and its relation to flame length.

Hawthorne's research at MIT was also in the area of secondary flow. Consider a river where the mass of the water is not in contact with any solid surfaces. This is the primary flow and may be easily described and modeled. But along the riverbed and the banks, where the flow is in contact with solid surfaces, the flow patterns are different. This is called secondary flow. When working with machinery such as gas turbines, it is very important to understand what type of secondary flow is occurring and what is causing it. By minimizing secondary flows, it is possible to improve the efficiency of such machinery.

Then it was back to England again. There had been an expansion of the Engineering Department at Cambridge University. Hawthorne was enticed to come back by his appointment as the first Hopkinson and ICI (Imperial Chemical Industries) Professor of Applied Thermodynamics. Aside from continuing his research, Hawthorne's efforts at Cambridge were also aimed at improving how thermodynamics was to be taught.

At this point, we have one more excursion back across the Atlantic. While retaining his position at Cambridge, Hawthorne returned to MIT for the 1955 – 1956 academic year as the first Jerome C. Hunsaker Visiting Professor of Aeronautical Engineering. Following the year at MIT, Hawthorne returned to Cambridge some months before the Suez Crisis occurred in late 1956.

Here I must discuss the one remaining interest of Hawthorne. He had an interest in science fiction that began with H. G. Wells. According to one source, he was for many years a subscriber to *Astounding Science Fiction*. This magazine was started as *Astounding Stories of Super-Science* in 1930. It still exists today as *Analog Science Fiction and Fact*. It is not known when Hawthorne first encountered *Astounding*. This might have been through the British version that existed from 1942 to 1963. I would consider it more likely, however, that he first came across the magazine during his time at MIT in the 1930s. One very important point of his interest in science fiction is that he would discuss with others the feasibility of ideas presented in the stories.

A year before the Suez Crisis, there appeared in *Astounding Science Fiction* the first installment of a serial by Frank Herbert (1920 – 1986), who is known to most people as the author of *Dune*. But in 1955, *Dune* was still a number of years in his future. The story that appeared was *Under Pressure*, his first novel to be published. It started in the November 1955 issue and concluded in the January 1956 issue.

Frank Herbert began working on his novel when he and his family were living in Santa Rosa, California and he was a reporter for the *Santa Rosa Press Democrat*. It is not clear exactly when during that time he started work on the novel. The Herbert family moved many times over the years. In the fall of 1953, they traveled to Mexico and settled in the village of Chapala, which is just a short distance south of Guadalajara. It is known that he was working on *Under Pressure* at that time.

The Herbert family returned to California at the end of 1953 when their funds ran low. He then obtained a job as a speechwriter on the staff of the Senator from Oregon, Guy Cordon. While working in Washington D.C., Herbert made extensive use of the Library of Congress. As a member of Cordon's staff, he was able to employ the Legislative Reference Service to obtain any book or document he desired. An article had to be written to show Cordon's views on certain topics. It fell upon Frank Herbert to write the article, "Undersea Riches for Everybody," which looked at the possibility of exploiting oil and gas by drilling below the ocean. The completed article was purchased by *Collier's* but never appeared in print. Cordon was turned out of office in the November 1954 election, and Herbert was out of a job.

The family was now living in the state of Washington in a beach cabin located between Seattle and Tacoma. He kept working on the novel and finished it in April 1955. It was quickly accepted by John W. Campbell Jr., editor of *Astounding Science Fiction*. Campbell offered four cents a word. As the length was 75,000 words, that meant $3,000 for Frank Herbert, less 10 percent to his literary agent Lurton Blassingame. Although he had written the story with the assumption that it would be published in three installments, Herbert also had to write synopses to appear at the beginning of the second and third installments.

The novel was also sold to Doubleday even before it appeared in *Astounding*. This sale resulted in another $3,600 coming to Herbert. He was required to suggest an alternative title as Doubleday wanted something other than *Under Pressure*. His suggestion, *The Dragon in the Sea*, was accepted. This new title was based on a quotation from the Book of Isaiah that was used within the novel. Once the deal was completed, Doubleday moved very quickly and had it ready for publication in February 1956, which was the month after the serialization had concluded in *Astounding*. An Avon paperback version, titled *21ˢᵗ Century Sub*, appeared in November 1956. The story also appeared in the British version of *Astounding Science Fiction*, running from April to June 1956.

At first glance, *Under Pressure* may seem to simply be a novel of undersea warfare. Submarines are involved, but there is much more going on. In this story, the Western Powers are still in conflict with the Eastern Powers. The West has an oil shortage and their solution is to steal oil from the Eastern Powers. A sub tug drills into oil reserves on the continental shelf and brings the oil back in a long plastic barge towed behind the sub tug. In this means of obtaining the oil, we see a possible influence of the article "Undersea Riches for Everybody" or at least the research material used in its preparation.

The last 20 such missions have failed to return and no one knows why. Ensign John Ramsey, an electronics specialist in the Bureau of Psychology, is to be inserted into the crew of the *Fenian Ram*, a sub tug scheduled for an upcoming mission. The *Fenian Ram* happens to need a replacement electronics officer for its crew of four since the last one suffered a "psychotic blowup." Ramsey's primary mission is to evaluate the psychological condition of the crew under the stress of the mission. He also has to figure out why the missions are failing.

The *Fenian Ram* succeeds in its mission and returns with its cargo of oil. Ramsey learns how the Eastern Powers destroyed the previous missions and also makes recommendations that should help improve the morale of the sub tug crews. The usual discussion of this story focuses on the stress that the crew members had to endure. I will simply repeat the statement made by others that the original title has two meanings: the physical pressure on the sub and the psychological pressure on the crew.

Any information that Herbert needed on submarines was obtained solely by research. Although he briefly served in the U.S. Navy during World War II, none of this service had any connection with submarines.

What really concerns us here is the means by which the oil is transported. In the very first chapter, the plastic barge used to transport the oil is mentioned and it is said that crews call it a *slug*. Just a few sentences later, we are told that "A slug will carry almost one hundred million barrels of oil."

Let us consider that figure for a moment. As I said at the beginning of the chapter, a barrel of oil is equivalent to 42 gallons. When describing the capacity of the slug, Herbert said "almost." Rather than try to determine what he meant, I will assume its capacity is exactly one hundred million barrels. This means that the capacity of the slug is 4.2 **billion** gallons.

A value of that size is difficult to evaluate. To help you understand, let us consider how much oil tankers of different sizes are capable of carrying. It is first necessary to explain the term Deadweight Tonnage, which could be abbreviated as DWT or d.w.t. This is a measure of how much the ship can carry. It is not related to the weight of the ship itself, except that a larger ship would have a larger DWT. The term is the sum of the weights of cargo, fuel, fresh water, ballast water, provisions, passengers, and crew. To convert to barrels or gallons, one must first calculate or estimate what percentage of the DWT is actually due to the cargo.

In the World War II era, the T2 tanker had a capacity of 16,500 DWT. By 1953, the *Tina Onassis* had a capacity of approximately 50,000 DWT. Over the years, the size of tankers continued to increase. Today the largest supertankers are the ULCC (Ultra Large Crude Carrier) class, with a capacity of 320,000 to 550,000 DWT. According to Wikipedia, the four largest ships in the world are of the TI Class of ULCCs: *TI Africa*, *TI Asia*, *TI Europe* and *TI Oceania*. The capacity of each is given as about 500,000 DWT. The available information also gives their capacity as slightly over 3,100,000 barrels.

Returning to *Under Pressure*, the capacity of the slug, given as one hundred million barrels, is therefore equivalent to about 32 supertankers of the TI class. One might think that Herbert chose a value that was unreasonably large. But consider that the Western Powers, even if they were not contemplating the disastrous loss rate mentioned at the beginning of the story, obviously expected to lose *some* sub tugs. In such a case, the objective would be to get as much oil back on any given mission as possible. Even though the sub tugs were nuclear powered, a lot of power would be needed to pull such a load.

What else did Herbert say about the slugs? After tapping the reservoir of oil and pumping for many hours, we then have:

Full slug. It stretched out on the bottom behind the *Ram*, turgid with its cargo, almost a mile long, held in delicate hydrostatic balance so that it would tow beneath the surface.

There he is again with the word "almost." For a rough calculation, I will assume that the slug length is a nice round number: 5,000 feet. Herbert said nothing about the cross section of the slug or any tapering at either end. For ease of calculation, I will consider the slug to be a simple cylinder.

$$V = 4.2 \text{ billion gallons} = 561,458,352 \text{ cubic feet} = \pi r^2 h$$
$$\text{where } h = 5000$$

$$r^2 = 35,743.55 \rightarrow r = 189 \text{ feet} \rightarrow \text{diameter} = 378 \text{ feet}$$
$$\text{for a ratio of 1 to 13.2}$$

This ratio can be seen in Figure 7. If both ends were tapered in the practical version of such a container, the diameter would have to increase slightly to compensate for the loss in volume.

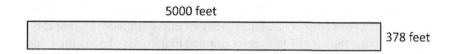

5000 feet

378 feet

Figure 7. Dimensions of slug.

To make another comparison with the supertankers, each member of the TI class is 1246 feet long with a beam (maximum width) of 223 feet. The length of the slug used in the calculations would have been less than 20 feet longer than <u>all four</u> of the TI class supertankers lined up bow to stern.

There is one other reference in *Under Pressure* to the size of the slug. As the *Fenian Ram* is proceeding to the enemy's oil field, it is said that "The six hundred feet of plastic barge trailing behind the *Ram* twisted, dragged, and skidded . . ." My interpretation is that this represents the empty slug in a folded or collapsed condition.

A few details about the slug as presented in *Under Pressure*. It was just not a simple container for the oil that was towed behind the sub tug. To be able to conform to the movements of the sub tug, it needed to be able to submerge, surface and adjust its depth on command. In the story, Herbert made reference to a compensator system and both bow and stern ballast tanks in the slug. All of these were under the control of the crew. If we are to consider the practicality of something like the slug, I think that such ballast tanks would have to be distributed along the entire length of the slug. Applying forces at only the bow and stern would have introduced stresses, possibly resulting in a rupture of the slug.

Herbert also introduced a novel type of ballast for the slug. On a conventional submarine, and of course the sub tug, the usual way to control depth is by adjusting the buoyancy using the ballast tanks. If the tanks are allowed to fill with sea water, the buoyancy is decreased and the submarine will sink lower in the water. If high-pressure air is used to force the water from the ballast tanks, the buoyancy is increased and the submarine will rise.

If we were to fill a slug with crude oil, it would float on the surface of the sea. This might not be true if the slug was made of metal, but Herbert has the slug made of some unidentified plastic. If you were to simply pump sea water into the ballast tanks of the slug, it would still float at or very near the surface. To make it submerge to the required depths you would have to introduce a material denser than water into the ballast tanks. And that is exactly what Herbert did – he used mud.

We now return to William Hawthorne shortly after the closure of the Suez Canal. Gasoline rationing had begun due to the shortfall in crude oil imports from the Middle East. According to Hawthorne, the search for the solution to the tanker problem began with two conversations that occurred on November 23, 1956. The first conversation was with J. C. S. Shaw, another member of the Engineering Department at Cambridge University. He discussed with Shaw the possibility of using a flexible plastic tube as an oil tanker. The second conversation was at luncheon with Sir Geoffrey Taylor, by then retired but best known for his work in fluid mechanics and wave theory. In his article "Sausages From High Table," Hawthorne related that:

> I do not remember whether it was the luncheon or the fleeting memory of a Science Fiction story I had read. I do remember asking my distinguished neighbour at High Table what he thought of the idea of filling plastic sausages with oil and towing them behind ships. His lively response fanned the spark, and we warmed ourselves at the flame for the rest of the meal.

As we know that he had already discussed the matter earlier that day with Mr. Shaw, we may safely discount the influence of the luncheon.

Initial calculations were performed on the basis of transporting 10,000 tons of oil. With that value as the starting point, there were a few important factors to consider. A vessel that was very long in relation to its diameter would probably be difficult to manage. If the vessel was made shorter, any increase in diameter would require that stronger materials be used. Hawthorne assumed a length of 600 feet. Assuming that the oil had a specific gravity of 0.85, he was easily able to calculate a diameter of about 30 feet, for a ratio of diameter to length of approximately 1 to 20. This ratio will also be given for various models to be described.

My reason for providing the information on the tests and experiments that were performed by Hawthorne and his team will be to show what is required to take such a basic idea as presented in a story and develop it into a practical system.

Within a few days, work had begun to pursue the idea. It was suggested that such a vessel would be composed of nylon or canvas with an inner lining of rubber or plastic. Based on the initial design, it was possible to calculate the magnitude of the stresses that would be encountered. Some very simple experiments were done with sausage skins and flexible rubber tubing. The sausage skins were found to be too stiff and were also attacked by the methylated spirits used to fill them. Based on the experiments done with the rubber tubing, it was then planned to construct two larger models. Model No. 1 was to be nine inches in diameter and 16 feet in length, which is a ratio of 1 to 21.3. Another proposed model was to be three feet in diameter and 60 feet long, a ratio of 1 to 20. The capacity of the second model was 10 tons.

A company was found to manufacture Model No. 1 and it was available in time for testing to start in January 1957 during the university vacation. Testing was performed in the towing tank at the National Physical Laboratory in Teddington. During the tests, Model No. 1 was filled with industrial alcohol diluted with water to give the same specific gravity as the oil to be transported. An unanticipated problem was observed during the tests. This was a buckling motion which was called snaking and is shown in Figure 8.

Figure 8. Model No. 1 showing snaking during tests in towing tank. (Reproduced by permission of the estate of Sir William Hawthorne.)

The appearance and degree of snaking depended on the pressure inside the model and the speed at which it was being towed. This was a serious problem that had to be analyzed and fixed as snaking had the potential of causing a rupture of the body and the loss of the cargo.

While these early experiments were going on, a name was suggested for the flexible barge. Andrew Sydenham Farrar Gow, a classical scholar and a Fellow of Trinity College, suggested the term Dracone. This was based on the Greek Δράκων, which it should be noted means *serpent* and not *dragon*.

The next large model to be constructed was three feet in diameter and 67 feet in length. This is a ratio of 1 to 22.3. It consisted of a tube 45 feet long with 11 foot sections at each end with an ellipsoidal taper. It could hold 10 tons of alcohol but only weighed 100 pounds when empty. This model was called *Draconella* when it was made ready for river testing. A shorter and slimmer model called *Draconeel* was obtained with the original plan to place it inside *Draconella* as a means of varying internal pressure during tests. Although this was done, *Draconeel* was eventually used on its own in towing tests.

As testing continued and additional models were proposed and constructed, the world tanker situation had changed. In April 1957, the Suez Canal was reopened and by May it was being predicted that there would soon be a surplus rather than a shortage of ocean-going tankers. The rationale for the development of a 10,000-ton version of the Dracone no longer existed. In September 1957, it was suggested that a smaller barge in the 10,000-gallon capacity range would find applications in areas of the world where acquiring such a flexible barge would be much cheaper than acquiring and using a conventional steel barge. In addition, designing a smaller barge would reduce the various stresses and forces to be encountered and simplify the search for suitable materials.

A number of models of differing size and capacity were developed in the first few years of the Dracone project. The basic dimensions of these early models are shown in Figure 9.

You will see from the table in Figure 9 that *Draconeel* is the slimmest one listed, with a diameter to length ratio of 1 to 44. Another source states that models were tested with ratios from that extreme down to one with a ratio of only 1 to 7. You can also see from the table that all of the other models had a diameter to length ratio in the neighborhood of 1 to 20. This value had emerged from the calculations for the original concept of a 10,000-ton version and is also very near to that of Model No. 1.

As I mentioned, one problem that was observed at the very beginning of tests was snaking. Another problem that only became apparent after models were placed in service was due to internal pressure waves when towing in rough seas. A pressure wave would travel towards the tail and cause it to become rigid. The periodic change of the tail from a relaxed

	D (ft.)	L(ft.)	α (ft.)	Capacity (gallons)	Empty weight (tons)	D / L Ratio
Draconella	3	67	11	2,800	0.05	1 / 22.3
Draconeel	1	44	3.3	240	--	1 / 44
D.1	4.8	100	17	9,820	1.15	1 / 20.8
F.1	7.0	137	21.8	28,820	2.5	1 / 19.6
K.1	10.2	206.5	35.9	90,300	6.5	1 / 20.2
B.1	4.0	68.2	12	4,585	0.5	1 / 17.1

state to rigid was given the name "tail flick." If the action was severe and prolonged, the internal lining of the Dracone would separate from the outer fabric and begin to tear. The liquid cargo would then leak through the fabric. A Dracone filled with approximately 400 tons of kerosene lost most of its cargo in rough weather due to this cause. Additional failures threatened to bring the entire project to an end.

First consider the problem of snaking. Many experiments were performed on the different models and much analysis was done. The problem was related to the stability of ships being towed and also to the behavior of lighter-than-air craft. Three potential solutions emerged from the tests and analysis.

The first solution involved hanging triangular fins of weighted wood or fabric below the Dracone. Results depended on size and placement of the fins. The second solution involved attaching a drogue – a cylindrical or cone shaped object acting like a small underwater parachute. This approach also worked, but the method of attaching the drogue to the tail of the dracone was critical. The third solution was based on a detailed analysis of the flow at the tail. It was found that if the tail was hemispherical instead of tapered, there would be no snaking. Squaring off the tail with a wooden disk gave the same effect. A ring stabilizer was then developed to fit around the tapered tail section. This caused a change in the flow pattern known as separation of flow, which stabilized the barge. The third solution was preferred to the first two since the fin and drogue were subject to damage by underwater obstacles. It was necessary to develop a stabilizer that would not increase the drag too much.

The tail flick problem was a bit harder to address. The solution appeared to be in the area of the fairings, where the fabric and lining were joined to the nose and tail end pieces. The descriptions of the problem only state that two approaches were taken. The first was to change the shape of the tail fairing to reduce the violent whipping action. The second approach was change the manufacturing process of the fairings to make them less susceptible to such damage.

Many of the tests of Dracones were performed in bodies of water in and around England. Additional Dracones that were constructed on the basis of the D.1 model were tested in various places around the world. This included locations in Africa, Malaya, Borneo, and Indonesia. They were also used in demonstrations that were given in locations such New York, Oslo and Montreal.

More than 60 years after the original discussion by William

Figure 9. Dimensions of various Dracone models. Based on a figure in "The Early Development of the Dracone Flexible Barge."

Hawthorne, Dracones are still being used around the world. In most cases, the purpose is as originally conceived: the transport of cargoes such as oil. It has also been used in the cleanup process following oil spills where a small vessel can pump large volumes of liquid into a Dracone which then transports it to a location for proper disposal. Another unanticipated application involves cruise ships. Large cruise ships must empty their bilge, waste water and sewage water. As an alternative to simply dumping such polluting material into the ocean, it can be loaded into Dracones for disposal. The Dracone has also been used to remove fuel from vessels damaged by shipwreck or natural disaster. In looking at the models available from one manufacturer, they range from one 28 feet in length with a capacity of only 1030 gallons to one 300 feet in length with a capacity of 247,000 gallons. One interesting feature is that many models continue to be manufactured with a diameter to length ratio near to 1 to 20.

One may locate patents in the name of William Hawthorne (usually in conjunction with others) both in Britain and the United States dealing with the basic concept of the Dracone and improvements to some detail of its construction or use. The important condition regarding the ability to obtain a patent in the case of the Dracones is Novelty. The concept of Novelty in the patent law of the United States will be discussed only briefly here; it will be considered in greater detail in Chapter 7.

You cannot obtain a patent on something that is previously known: something that is not Novel. If a description of a device or system has appeared in a publication, it might not be possible to obtain a patent at some later date. Such a description usually means in a technical publication but may also refer to works of fiction. How would it then have been possible to obtain patents for the Dracone given the publication of *Under Pressure*?

To prevent the patent from being issued, what is described in the publication must correspond exactly with whatever the attempt is made to patent at a later date. We know there is one basic difference between the slug and the Dracone: the slug had the ability to operate submerged and the Dracone does not. In addition, the description must be such that a person having ordinary skill in the art should be able to make the invention without the need for undue subsequent research and experimentation. It should be clear from even the limited description that I have provided of the activities of Hawthorne and his colleagues that this was definitely not the case.

The brief discussion of patents enables me to correct an erroneous statement that appears in *Dreamer of Dune*. Brian Herbert said that when

Frank Herbert learned of the Dracone, he was advised to take action to try to invalidate the patents. According to Brian Herbert:

> Dad consulted a number of people on this, including John W. Campbell, and learned from them, to his dismay, that he should have filed formal patent papers within two years of publication of his idea. The publication gave him "discovery rights" for that period, but his failure to file proper documents sent the idea into the public domain.

First of all, there is no such thing as "discovery rights." Second, the time limit between making an invention known and the application for the patent was, at that time, limited to one year and not two. Third, if Herbert had attempted to file for a patent based on the story, it would have most likely been for an underwater barge such as the slug. Fourth, I doubt that Frank Herbert would have had the technical knowledge to convert a story concept into a patent. Finally, even if he had been able to obtain a patent on something resembling the slug that operated submerged, would it have had any relevance to a barge such as the Dracone that operated on the surface?

Of course, there was more to the rest of the life of William Hawthorne than the Dracone. At MIT, he was made a Visiting Institute Professor in 1962 and a member of the MIT Corporation from 1969 to 1974. Back in England, he was the head of the Engineering Department at Cambridge from 1968 to 1973. In 1968 he also became Master of the newly created Churchill College, a position he retained until 1983.

William Hawthorne was a member of a number of engineering societies. He received awards and honors for his accomplishments, both in Britain and in the United States. He was made a Commander of the Order of the British Empire in 1959. He was then knighted for "services to thermodynamics" in 1970. He was elected Fellow of the Royal Society in 1955 and served as its vice president from 1969 to 1970 and again from 1979 to 1981.

Let us finally return to the question of inspiration of Hawthorne by a work of science fiction. I must first clear up some errors that exists in the literature. The Dracone was called a "flexible undersea oil barge" by Timothy O'Reilly in *Frank Herbert*, a "flexible underwater barge" by Brian Herbert in *Dreamer of Dune* and a "flexible submarine tanker" by Arthur C. Clarke in *Profiles of the Future*. This is taking the connection with the slug of Frank Herbert's story too far. One only has to look over the available information to realize that the Dracone has none of the features of the slug, such as ballast tanks, that would be necessary for it to run submerged. Another mistake was made by Clarke when referring to Herbert's story, as he said that the submarine was towing a "string of submersible oil-barges."

In the story related by Hawthorne about luncheon at High Table at Trinity College, he just referred to some unnamed science fiction story. We have a similar statement by way of Arthur C. Clarke in *Profiles of the Future*. He states that the inventor of the Dracone (unnamed, but we know who) said "I got the idea from a science-fiction story." Clarke then assumes it was from *The Dragon in the Sea*.

The best evidence I have been able find comes from the text of a talk titled simply "Dracones" given by Hawthorne in June 1960 and then marked "Modified for August 1960." It is a marketing talk, but it is not known to which organization he was speaking in either case. Only the text has survived and not the various slides to which he referred. At the beginning of the talk, he says that the concept of using plastic or flexible vessels to transport liquids is described in science fiction stories. After giving many details of the development work, he stated:

> During the early part of this lecture I mentioned that flexible barges made of plastic have been the subject of science fiction stories. In the next slide I reproduce an illustration of a science fiction story published in 1955 which I think you will agree is a very imaginative, an almost Jules Verne prediction, or forerunner of the Dracone vessel I have been describing. In fact, the science fiction story, of which this in an illustration, described the towing of oil by submarines in plastic barges.

It is clear by the reference to the towing of the barge by submarines that Hawthorne meant *Under Pressure* and the date of publication clearly points to *Astounding Science Fiction* as published in the United States. This would point to him encountering the story while at MIT as the Hunsaker Visiting Professor. Prior to the discovery of this document, it was not possible to determine which version of the story he encountered. The dates of publication of the hardback and the British issues of *Astounding* in which the story appeared occurred before the November 1956 conversations. Even the paperback version that came out in November had to be considered as the possible source.

Although no simple and unambiguous statement directly from Sir William Hawthorne to the effect that he was inspired by the concept of the slug as presented in *Under Pressure* has been located, I maintain that sufficient evidence has been presented here to confirm such inspiration.

6

A DUSTY TRAIL

The problem was deciding how nuclear fission should be used in warfare.

In Chapter 3, which looked at the writings of H. G. Wells and the ideas of Leo Szilard, I took the story to the point where fission in uranium had been discovered by Hahn and Strassmann and explained by Meitner and Frisch. In this chapter, I will pick up the story at that point and attempt to show how a science fiction story may have had a minor influence on the chain of decisions that led to the development of the atomic bomb by the United States.

It was realized that the discovery of fission in uranium suggested the possibility that it could be used for peaceful purposes and in warfare. I must emphasize the word "possibility" as many of the facts regarding fission were unknown at that time. Many experiments had to be performed and their results carefully interpreted before things became clearer.

Before proceeding, I must provide a very brief (I promise!) physics lesson. I am placing it here so that you will have a better understanding of what will follow.

In Chapter 3, I pointed out that it was recognized that an atom containing a number of negative electrons must be balanced by a positive charge of equal magnitude. It was not possible to develop a model of the atom that matched the facts until the existence of the neutron was first proposed and then confirmed. The neutron is neither negative nor positive, so it does not affect the overall electric charge of the atom. As the neutron was the central point of the ideas put forward by Szilard, I did not say much more about atomic structure at that time.

In *almost* any atom, we have a nucleus composed of protons and neutrons. (The nucleus of ^{1}H, the most common form of hydrogen, contains just one proton. The nucleus of ^{2}He, a type of helium, contains just two protons.) Since we are interested in the fission of the uranium nucleus, let us look at the structure of the uranium atom.

In uranium, the number of protons in the nucleus is 92. If the number of protons was not 92, it would not be uranium; it would be the nucleus of some other element. The number of electrons matches, as in any element, the number of protons; so we also have 92 electrons.

You can have multiple forms of a given element, by varying the number of neutrons in the nucleus. These different forms of an element are called isotopes. In uranium, there are three naturally occurring isotopes: ^{234}U, ^{235}U and ^{238}U. The number associated with any nucleus, called the atomic weight, is the sum of the number of protons and the number of neutrons. This tells us that nuclei of each of the isotopes of uranium must contain either 142 neutrons or 143 neutrons or 146 neutrons.

I will conclude the physics discussion with two very important details. First, the most common isotope is ^{238}U, which is approximately 99.3% of natural uranium. Second, the chemical properties of any element are determined by the number of electrons. Such minor variations in properties that might exist between isotopes are more pronounced in a light element such as hydrogen and are of no consequence in a heavy element such as uranium. This means that you cannot separate the isotopes of uranium by any chemical process.

I will begin by presenting the lives of two physicists, one very well-known and the other a bit more obscure.

The more prominent physicist was Ernest Orlando Lawrence (1901 – 1958). He was born in Canton, South Dakota. As a minor detail, Lawrence's childhood friend Merle Tuve lived across the street and was exactly six weeks older. Tuve also had a distinguished career in physics and was the founding director of The Johns Hopkins University Applied Physics Laboratory in 1942. Both were of Norwegian immigrant background.

Lawrence's first college experience was a disaster. At his mother's insistence, he was sent to St. Olaf College in Northfield, Minnesota. The conditions imposed at this Lutheran institution were such that he wound up getting very low grades in most subjects. He enrolled in the University of South Dakota in Vermillion for his sophomore year and *then* informed his parents. One of the faculty at USD, Lewis Akeley, was impressed with Lawrence and convinced him to switch his major from pre-med to physical sciences.

He received his bachelor of science degree in 1922. He then went to the University of Minnesota to begin his graduate work. Lawrence came under influence of William Swann, another faculty member who had an effect on the course of his life. Swann's approach was counter to that of many faculty who focused on teaching just the facts of a subject such as physics. His interest was in stimulating the creativity of the student.

Lawrence's mechanical skills were applied to investigating a phenomenon of electromagnetism. The results obtained were sufficient for his master's thesis, which also appeared as his first published paper, "The charging effect produced by the rotation of a prolate iron spheroid in a uniform magnetic field."

Swann then moved to the University of Chicago and then to Yale University, followed by Lawrence. At Yale, Lawrence performed the research that led to him receiving his Ph.D. in 1925. His dissertation was "The photo-electric effect in potassium vapour as a function of the frequency of the light." After receiving his Ph.D., Lawrence remained at Yale, first as a research fellow and then as an assistant professor. He continued to experiment and publish, being noted both for the topics he investigated and for his experimental approaches.

Lawrence wished to move higher at Yale, but they refused to consider a promotion to associate professor for one so young. This led him to accept an offer in 1928 from the University of California at Berkeley. After being at Berkeley a short time, he began work on the device that would establish his reputation and win him a Nobel Prize.

The primary means of learning about the structure of the atom was to bombard it, meaning the nucleus of the atom, with some particle. The results of the bombardment, when properly interpreted, would hopefully lead to an advance in understanding. In fact, the concentration of the positive charge of the atom into a compact nucleus was discovered by Rutherford in this manner. The particle used in these early tests was the alpha particle. An alpha particle consists of two protons and two neutrons and is therefore identical to the nucleus of a helium atom.

Alpha particles are usually obtained from the radioactive elements including, but not limited to, uranium and radium. A source of particles for many of the early atomic experiments was a vial containing a tiny amount of some compound of radium. A laboratory that had a sample of this rare and expensive element was indeed fortunate. With a natural source, however, the experimenter was limited by the energy of the emitted particles and their concentration.

The search began in the 1920s to find means of accelerating subatomic particles to high velocities. This would enable the particles to be used in ways not possible with natural sources. The conventional view was that high voltages, at least on the order of 1 million volts, were needed. How does one generate such a voltage and apply it when and where it was needed? This led to some quite interesting approaches, involving Tesla coils, van de Graaff generators and even a German attempt to harness lightning (two of the three members of the German team managed to survive the experiment).

Others tried approaches that were not so dangerous or difficult. If some way could be found to apply smaller accelerating forces again and again, then very high velocities could be reached without the need for very high voltages. One approach was the linear accelerator, where the particles are accelerated in steps as they proceed down a long tube.

Then there was the approach developed by Lawrence. You begin with a short metal cylinder, a drum. Cut this cylinder in half so that you have two pieces shaped like the letter D. (In discussions of cyclotrons, these pieces are called *Dees*.) The two Dees are placed in a vacuum chamber, as you do not want the particles you are accelerating to collide with air molecules. There is a small gap between the Dees.

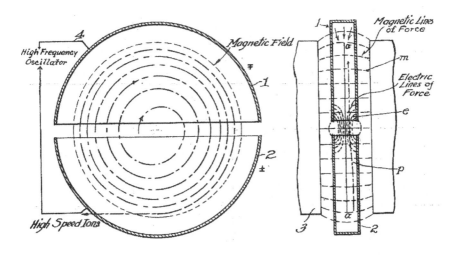

Figure 10. Diagram of Cyclotron. Taken from Lawrence's patent 1,948,384.

This is now placed between the poles of a large magnet. The Dees would be in the horizontal plane with the pole pieces of the magnet above and below. In Figure 10, the second part of the diagram shows the Dees rotated into a vertical orientation so that the pole pieces are to the left and right. The magnetic field passes through the Dees. Particles injected near the center will move on a curved path under the influence of the magnetic field.

Now comes the important part. A high-frequency oscillator is connected to the two Dees. The frequency of the oscillator is chosen so that a particle will make one trip around the chamber during a single cycle of the oscillator output. As the particle passes from one Dee to the other after half a cycle, the electric field between the field has now reversed so that the particle is accelerated in the proper direction. This kick is applied again and again, every half cycle.

As the particle accelerates, the radius of the path increases, becoming a spiral. Finally, the particle is moving so fast it is at the outer edge of the chamber, where it may be deflected for some useful purpose. The frequency used to accelerate a particle is based on the magnetic field strength, and the particle's mass and electric charge. This frequency is independent of the radius of the orbit.

Work was begun by Lawrence and his graduate student M. Stanley Livingston in the fall of 1930. The first chamber built by Livingston seemed almost a toy, only 4 inches in diameter. Inconclusive results were obtained in December of that year. During the Christmas holiday, it was possible for Livingston to borrow a more powerful magnet. With the oscillator at slightly less than 1000 volts, he was able to get particles at 80,000 volts. This means each particle had made 41 revolutions, obtaining the accelerating kick at 82 crossing of the gap between the Dees. This was sufficient for Livingston to obtain his Ph.D.

Many problems had to be investigated and fixes developed to obtain clearer evidence that the device was operating as designed. Wire grids covering the openings to the Dees were removed. The electric fields at the edges then acted as lenses to help keep particles in the proper plane. Another problem arose because of irregularities in the field of the magnet. These were cured by using shims: pieces of iron foil shaped like tears or exclamation marks. The shims were placed at various locations between the pole faces and the vacuum chamber. It was a tedious trial and error method to obtain the required uniformity of field, but by January 1932 they were able to announce they had obtained protons at 1.22 MeV with an oscillator operating at only 4,000 volts. The term *cyclotron* began as Laboratory slang and then became the official name in 1936.

The Radiation Laboratory was established in August 1931. The Laboratory began to build bigger and bigger cyclotrons. The two determining factors of the possible particle energy are the strength of the magnetic field and the radius of the chamber. The maximum strength of field from an iron core electromagnet is about 2 Tesla (1 T = 1 Tesla = 10,000 Gauss, where the strength of the Earth's magnetic field at its surface is between 0.25 and 0.65 Gauss). To obtain higher energies, it became clear that cyclotrons (and their magnets) had to be made larger. By 1932, there was a cyclotron with a diameter of 27 inches. By 1937, they were up to 37 inches, and then 60 inches by 1939. The completion of a 184-inch unit was delayed by World War II. It was completed in 1946 as a newer type of particle accelerator.

During the 1930s, other Colleges and Universities and other nations also made efforts to construct their own cyclotrons. Many of these efforts had the assistance of people from Berkeley. But Lawrence and his team at Berkeley always stayed ahead of everyone else. The funding to construct larger and larger devices had to be obtained during the 1930s, when the United States was still in the grips of the Great Depression. You can clearly point to Lawrence's scientific accomplishments, and the fact that he received the Nobel Prize in Physics in November 1939 for the invention of the cyclotron. We must not neglect, however, his demonstrated talents as a fund raiser.

We will now leave Lawrence and look at the lesser-known physicist I mentioned earlier.

Robert Alden Cornog (1912 – 1998) was born in Portland, Oregon. His birthdate was July 7; I will explain the significance of that date in a bit. His father Jacob was a graduate student in chemistry at Oregon State University, which was then called the Oregon Agricultural College. At that time, one of his teaching assistants was Linus Pauling. During World War I, Jacob worked as a chemist in New York City. After the war, Jacob continued his graduate studies at Ohio State. Upon obtaining his Ph.D., he became a faculty member at University of Iowa in Iowa City. This is where Robert Cornog grew up.

Although he had an interest in becoming a physicist, Cornog followed his father's advice and got his bachelor's degree in mechanical engineering from the University of Iowa. He signed up to do graduate work in physics there, but then changed his mind and applied for a government job. This job was with the U.S. Bureau of Reclamation in Denver. Part of his work involved analysis of components of Boulder Dam and gave him real-world engineering experience.

During his time in Denver, Cornog met Robert Heinlein. This was at the Denver Athletic Club, where Heinlein was judging a fencing contest. Heinlein had developed tuberculosis while serving in the Navy. He had been treated at the Fitzsimmons Army Hospital in Denver and would eventually be required to retire from the Navy. The sport in which Heinlein had excelled at the Naval Academy was fencing, so he was well qualified to judge the match in Denver. They discovered that they shared the same birthday, although Heinlein was five years older.

After some time with the Bureau of Reclamation, Cornog had decided that he wanted to get back to physics. But on the recommendation of his mother and others, he stayed on the government job in Denver for two years. He was able to save his money and so had a thousand dollars when he left the job. Cornog's college physics instructor, Alexander Ellett, suggested that he should become an experimental physicist and that the best place to go was Berkeley to study under Lawrence.

Cornog applied to Berkeley and was accepted. When he arrived there in the fall of 1935, he ran into some difficulties. With his background in engineering, he had never taken some of the required prerequisite courses for graduate work in physics. His efforts during his first year included taking the required courses and in general bringing himself up to the proper level of understanding.

Lawrence obtained some of the funding for the construction of larger cyclotrons by stating that they could be used to advance medical knowledge. By bombarding a particular element with alpha particles or protons or deuterons (one proton and one neutron; the nucleus of ^{2}H, deuterium), it was possible to artificially create new isotopes. A radioactive isotope of a useful element could be tracked in the body before its level of radiation decayed. One such isotope is radiosodium, which was made at Berkeley by bombarding ordinary table salt with deuterons. This converted some of the normal ^{23}Na atoms to the radioactive isotope ^{24}Na.

Many hours of cyclotron operation were devoted to the creation of suitable quantities of radiosodium and other useful isotopes. But it was still possible to make important scientific discoveries. One of these discoveries involved Robert Cornog.

The discovery focused on the isotopes of hydrogen and helium. Most of the hydrogen that exists is ^{1}H, with only a proton in its nucleus. Then ^{2}H, deuterium, was discovered. It is stable like the more common isotope and has one proton and one neutron in its nucleus. But what can be said about ^{3}H?

Then there is helium. The most common isotope of helium is ^{4}He, with two protons and two neutrons in its nucleus. Remember that such a nucleus is identical with an alpha particle. We can speak of ^{2}He, which has only two protons in its nucleus. If it exists, it is considered extremely unstable. But what about ^{3}He?

Researchers in Britain had obtained results that indicated the existence of nuclei of either ^{3}H or ^{3}He. The nature of their experiments did not make it possible to decide one way or the other. Others attempted to isolate sufficient quantities of either isotope to solve the problem but were also unsuccessful. All sorts of arguments went back and forth between physicists. It was generally accepted, however, that ^{3}He was radioactive and ^{3}H was stable. According to Hans Bethe, any ^{3}He in nature should have decayed away and none would be found.

Then Luis Alvarez (1911 – 1988) entered the picture. Alvarez received the Nobel Prize in Physics in 1968 for his work in elementary particle physics. He is perhaps better known to the public for the hypothesis developed along with his son Walter that the extinction of the dinosaurs was caused by the impact of a large asteroid on the Earth.

In 1936, Alverez obtained his Ph.D. in physics from the University of Chicago. Looking for a job, he asked his sister Gladys, who happened to be a part-time secretary for Ernest Lawrence, if there were any positions available at the Radiation Laboratory. A telegram soon arrived with a job offer. Over the years that followed, Alvarez gained much experience with the Berkeley cyclotrons. One of his first important jobs was in designing the magnet for the 60-inch cyclotron.

In July 1939, Alvarez had the idea to accelerate deuterons into a deuterium target using the 37-inch cyclotron to see if he could create some material of mass 3. This would then be fed into the 60-inch cyclotron. By adjusting the magnetic field so that it would accelerate ^{3}He ions, he could obtain an indication of their presence with his ionization chamber. The first step was simply to test his chamber with the 60-inch cyclotron. If too many other extra ions were detected by the chamber in advance of running their experiment, it would not be possible to make the proposed test.

Alvarez enlisted Cornog's help in moving the ionization chamber from the 37-inch cyclotron to the 60-inch cyclotron. Cornog then disappeared for a few hours to participate in a track meet. The cyclotron contained a quantity of helium from an underground well. Alvarez was able to see indications of deuterons and normal helium (^{4}He) ions and, of greater importance, saw no indication of extra ions that would mask the ^{3}He ions in the proposed experiment. At the conclusion of the experiment, Alvarez told the operator to take the magnetic field up to the normal value and then shut everything down. The normal procedure is to cut the oscillator power first and then cut the power to the magnets. This time the power to the magnets was turned off first.

As the magnetic field collapsed, Alvarez saw a burst of particles on the oscilloscope screen. He asked the operators to power up the magnets and tried it again. The point at which he saw the burst corresponded to ^{3}He. When Cornog returned from the track meet, Alvarez told him of the result. It was realized that the collapsing magnetic field set up conditions in the poles of the magnets such that the cyclotron was momentarily tuned for

^{3}He. After Alvarez and Cornog made the necessary adjustments to the 60-inch cyclotron, they were able to obtain a steady beam of ^{3}He ions.

Remember that these results were obtained with the gas from the underground well, not with anything made using the 37-inch cyclotron. If ^{3}He was radioactive as predicted, it should have all decayed away in the millions of years the gas was underground. This meant that ^{3}He is actually stable. Alvarez said that he was ashamed to admit that it took him a week to realize that this implied that ^{3}H was radioactive.

Cornog took over and performed the next series of experiments. By bombarding deuterium gas with deuterons as originally planned, they obtained a mixture of gases that was radioactive. This mixture was then processed to give a final result that they could guarantee was pure hydrogen gas. But this end result was still radioactive, which meant that the source of radioactivity was ^{3}H.

In his tests, Cornog obtained too high an estimate for the rate of decay (too small of a value for the half-life) of ^{3}H. His result was affected by an infinitesimal leak in a section of rubber tubing in his equipment. He was not just measuring the radioactive decay of ^{3}H; he was also measuring the loss of ^{3}H through the leak. The results of these experiments, however, were sufficient for Cornog to write his Ph.D. dissertation "Hydrogen and Helium of Mass Three," dated December 1939.

We are now at the end of 1939. We shall leave Lawrence with his Nobel Prize and Robert Cornog with his Ph.D. and move over to science fiction.

At the end of 1939, the leading pulp science fiction magazine was *Astounding Science-Fiction*. John W. Campbell, Jr. (1910 – 1971) had been named assistant editor in October 1937.

As a young boy, Campbell had been the type we seem to encounter quite a bit in these chapters. He read books on science, performed chemistry experiments at home and did the usual mechanical tinkering. His reading also included fiction, such as the work of Edgar Rice Burroughs. Campbell also became familiar with the writing of Jules Verne and H. G. Wells. This may have been while he was a young child, but definitely when he encountered the first issue of *Amazing Stories* in 1926.

Campbell began as a student at MIT in 1928. Shortly thereafter, he began writing science fiction. He submitted two stories to *Amazing Stories* and both were purchased. Wondering why the first story had not appeared, he went to see the editor, T. O'Conor Sloane. He was told by Sloane that the manuscript to the first story, "Invaders from the Infinite," had been lost. Campbell did not possess a carbon copy of that story, so his first published work was his second sale, "When the Atoms Failed."

Campbell continued to write and sell stories, which appeared in *Amazing Stories* and *Amazing Stories Quarterly*. But, it appears that he was devoting too much time to writing science fiction. He had to leave MIT at the end of his junior year in 1931. He was unable to satisfy the necessary language requirement since he failed German. We may only speculate how much his other grades were also affected by his writing activities. Campbell went on to obtain his bachelor's degree in physics from Duke University in 1933.

For the next few years, Campbell continued to write and establish himself as an author. Unfortunately, it was a bit of a struggle. He had to support a wife, having married Dona Stuart in 1931. What money there was came from a succession of low-paying jobs, supplemented by the income from the sales of his stories.

This all changed in 1937. There was a management shuffle at Street & Smith, the publisher of *Astounding Stories*. F. Orlin Tremaine, who had been the editor of *Astounding Stories* since the end of 1933, was moved to a position which placed him in charge of multiple magazines. In late 1937, Campbell was hired as assistant editor of *Astounding Stories*, working under Tremaine. In May 1938, Campbell became the man in charge of *Astounding Science-Fiction*. The change of the title from *Astounding Stories* took effect with the March 1938 issue.

Campbell was fascinated by science and all sorts of technical and scientific advances. During his many years as editor, this sometimes led him to present and promote unproven claims or even pseudoscientific concepts. Campbell would present his views in his editorials and in articles that usually appeared under a pseudonym. One topic in which he had a great interest was the promise of the power of the atom. In the June 1938 issue of *Astounding*, his editorial "Fantastic Fiction" contained the following statement:

> But you can be fairly certain of this: **the discoverer of the secret of atomic power is alive on Earth today**. His papers and researches are appearing regularly; his name is known. But the exact handling of the principles he's discovered – not even he knows now. We don't know which is his name.
>
> But we know him. **He's here today**.

Following the discovery of fission in uranium, Campbell wrote three articles presenting the facts as they were then known and understood. All of these appeared as by Arthur McCann, a pseudonym that he used for a total of 21 science articles, and also for a number of letters in the "Brass

Tacks" section of the magazine. The articles were "Isotope 235" in the August 1939 issue, "Atomic Ringmaster" in the March 1940 issue and "Shhhhh – Don't Mention It!" in the August 1940 issue.

"Isotope 235" was very short, covering only two pages. Campbell's explanation of how the nuclei behaved during fission is confused, which is understandable given the general level of knowledge at that time. His most obvious error was in stating that the ^{235}U is present only as 1 part in 1000 in natural uranium, where the correct value is about 1 part in 140. The article is interesting as it points out the two methods that might be employed for the separation of isotopes are diffusion and by employing the principle of the mass spectrograph. Both of these methods were employed by the Manhattan Project.

"Atomic Ringmaster" is of interest here only because it also mentions the separation of ^{235}U from ^{238}U. The bulk of the article discussed another possible technique for the separation of atoms and even complex molecules based on work being done by Isidor I. Rabi at Columbia University.

Before moving to the third McCann article, it is useful to consider some letters exchanged between Campbell and the author Robert A. Heinlein. His first published story "Life-Line" had appeared in the August 1939 issue of *Astounding*. Heinlein was beginning to establish quite a reputation with his early stories.

The first letter was from Campbell, dated January 15, 1940. He said that he had been talking to people at Columbia University who were involved in nuclear research. He came away with some information on cyclotrons and atomic power and the idea for a story. The problem would be one of control of a nuclear reaction. Campbell assumed that the reaction would proceed so quickly that the operators would never be able to react in time to prevent a disaster. The strain would be such that it would eventually drive the operators mad.

Heinlein's response, dated January 20, told Campbell of a visit by a friend who just happened to be at Berkeley, Robert Cornog. He provided Heinlein with technical information very similar to that obtained by Campbell. Heinlein said that he would like to start working on the story, but that he needed more information on the physics and asked Campbell to recommend some books on the subject.

Campbell replied that if both he and Cornog were having the same thoughts on the subject, it was a sign that the matter should be pursued. With regard to Heinlein's request for books, Campbell had to say that there weren't any. Things in that field were changing rapidly and the books had to catch up. Any book that took many months to prepare ran the risk of having much of the material proved untrue by the time it was ready to be published. He suggested that Heinlein's best source for such information would be his physicist friend.

At the end of January, Heinlein wrote that he had started working on the uranium story. He sent it to Campbell on February 23. Heinlein said that he had originally intended to send it to Cornog for a final technical review, but thought it was best to get it to Campbell as quickly as possible. Such technical details that he found necessary to include were presented in a way to prevent the story from "blowing up in our faces." The story, "Blowups Happen," was immediately accepted by Campbell but did not appear until the September issue of *Astounding*.

Articles on the state of atomic research were appearing in the newspapers. On May 5, the *New York Times* had an article on atomic power by William Laurence. Compared with what we know now, there were some technical errors in the article. Many of the errors could be due to the material available to Laurence at the time or his unfamiliarity with the topic. Generally speaking, it was a very good article. It explained about the isotopes of uranium and the need the separate them, the amount of energy possible and that the energy release could be either explosive or more gradual for use in power generation and propulsion.

The article was so positive on the topic that it apparently left many people with the impression that atomic power was right around the corner. Another article was published in the *Times* on May 12. This article, by Waldemar Kaempffert, pointed out the problem preventing the immediate appearance of atomic power was the need to separate the isotopes of uranium. Only incredibly small quantities of ^{235}U had been separated so far using the mass spectrographic method. The readers, Kaempffert noted, should not expect oil or coal to be replaced anytime soon.

Now we come to Campbell's third article on fission, "Shhhhh – Don't Mention It!" He began by referring to a recent newspaper article that gave an extremely upbeat view of the possibilities of atomic power. I think that it is clear that he is referring to the May 5 *New York Times* article or one based upon it. Campbell said that his article would attempt to provide a more balanced analysis.

One way to look at the *Astounding* article is to consider what he got right and what he got wrong. He pointed out the need to separate the ^{235}U from the more abundant ^{238}U and that it was impossible to do so by chemical means. This led to a discussion of the mass spectrographic method and the tiny amounts that had been separated by that method. He also identified the locations of known uranium deposits – the Belgian Congo, Canada, Austria and Colorado.

His article contained the incorrect statement that ^{235}U would only fission with slow neutrons. This statement also appeared in the May 12

Times article and represented the state of knowledge at the time, so we might forgive him on this point. He then used the wrong approach in calculating the amount of radiation shielding that would be required for a reactor. This led him to conclude that it would have to be placed inside a mountain. This error was quickly noted in a letter to Heinlein and then corrected by Campbell using a letter from "Arthur McCann" in the October issue.

Regarding the use of ^{235}U in warfare, Campbell made the statement that "All U-235 will do is boil water." He said that all you could possibly make was a feeble steam bomb. This seems strange given his discussion with people at Columbia earlier in the year and the statements in newspaper articles about the possible large energy releases.

It is the suggestion he then made regarding the use of radioactive material in time of war that is of greatest interest to us:

> Story goes, the Romans conquered Carthage once or twice, and had to do it over again each time. They finally fixed that by leveling the city, then plowing salt into the fields around so that nothing could grow. That time Carthage stayed conquered. The modern equivalent would probably be to bomb the undesired city with a few pounds of a long-lived radioactive isotope. There would undoubtedly be plant life left—rather weird stuff, probably—but humans would find it expedient to get out and stay out for one hundred years or so. A few uranium power plants could easily manufacture the necessary isotope bombs.

I had made use of this quote before, and never thought much about the historical accuracy of Campbell's statements regarding Carthage. This turns out to be one of those things that everyone knows but that is not correct. An article in *Classical Philology* from 1986 tried to trace the origin of the salt story. To the author's surprise, it does not appear in works by any Roman authors such as Polybius, Livy, Scipio, Cicero and Macrobius. They might speak of the destruction visited upon Carthage or that the soil was cursed, but there was never any specific mention of salt. The earliest specific reference to salt and Carthage does not occur until 1930 when B. Hallward wrote in the *Cambridge Ancient History*:

> Buildings and walls were razed to the ground; the plough passed over the site, and salt was sown into the furrows made.

There is no indication of the source for Hallward's statement. The author of the *Classical Philology* article points out the only references to sowing with salt come from Jewish, Hittite and Assyrian texts that have nothing to do with Carthage.

We can only speculate where Campbell obtained his "fact" about Carthage. It may have been during his college days at either MIT or Duke or from a later source that derived from the *Cambridge Ancient History*. What is important is that Campbell took what he had learned about Carthage, however incorrect, and came up with a new idea based on radioactive material. He presented this in the *Astounding* article and also in an idea for a story he suggested to Heinlein.

In a letter from Heinlein to Campbell and his wife dated December 1, 1940 he said:

> I've just reread John's letter of November 12th. It would have been more appropriate six days earlier---Guy Fawkes day. Such nice ideas he has, radioactive dust to wipe out all of modern civilization.

The problem is that there is no letter from Campbell dated November 12 in the Heinlein Archives. There is, however, a letter which contains an outline for a long story involving radioactive dust. This letter only bears the typed header of "Monday" and a handwritten notation "Circa Dec 15, 1940." It is so clearly the letter to which Heinlein referred.

The time frame of Campbell's outline is from 1941 through 1977. In 1944, Berlin is dusted with "artificial radioactive ash." This is followed by Munich, Rome and other German and Italian cities. The war apparently ends, but a small group of Nazis learn how to make the dust and apply the same treatment to London and other English cities. There are Communist revolts in England and European countries. Dusting also occurs in the United States and Soviet Union.

Major cities are rendered uninhabitable. The conclusion of the outline in 1977 focuses on the question of how society will exist in such a decentralized state. During all of this dust warfare over the course of more than 30 years, the world population has been reduced by 75 percent.

In a letter dated December 17, Heinlein told Campbell that he was working on the radioactive dust story and expected to finish it before the week was out. He submitted the story on December 24 with the title "Foreign Policy." A suggested alternative title was "Pax Americana." Heinlein made use of only the very start of Campbell's outline, with the explanation that it could have required multiple novels to tell the full chain of events suggested by Campbell.

Campbell's reaction to the story was that it seemed weak and that the proposed solution was synthetic and unsatisfactory. He then proposed turning the apparent weakness of the story into its strength. The title would be changed to "Solution Unsatisfactory" and that he would promote the situation in the story as being highly probable and asking if the reader could suggest a better solution.

Heinlein agreed with Campbell's evaluation of the story. He intended the solution to be weak as the political problem imposed by the use of radioactive dust did not have a solution that would permit an advanced culture to continue to exist. Heinlein approved of the title change and suggested trying to get a discussion going for several months on the basis of letters submitted by readers. There were some suggested changes by Campbell after the story was purchased. Most of these changes were acceptable to Heinlein, except one that both he and his wife Leslyn thought destroyed the dramatic punch of the ending. An exchange of letters placed the ending in a form acceptable to both.

The premise of "Solution Unsatisfactory" was that the United States was not yet involved in the war but was attempting to develop an atomic bomb. It is explained that there was trouble developing a bomb that was stable enough to go off only when intended and have only the amount of explosive force intended. These problems were circumvented by the discovery that the material resulting from the processing of the uranium for the bomb was highly radioactive.

The lab doing the processing was located in Maryland. It was realized that radioactive material was being flushed into Chesapeake Bay and was killing fish. The decision was made to abandon work on the bomb and develop the radioactive dust as a weapon. It was then decided by the United States and Britain to use the dust in an attack on Berlin.

All of this was accomplished by Clyde Manning, a Congressman and former military officer. He was recalled to active duty at the start of the story and placed in charge of the project at the time when there was still a struggle to develop a bomb. After the attack on Berlin, it was realized by Manning that it was necessary for the United States to impose the necessary controls to prevent the dust process from being developed and employed by other nations. Before this could be successfully accomplished, there was a short dust war between the United States and the Eurasian Union, the successor to the Soviet Union. The story ends with the establishment of the Peace Patrol under the control of Commissioner Manning. This made Manning the military dictator of the world. The question posed at the conclusion of the story by Manning's assistant was "What happens when Manning dies?"

In his 1957 essay, "Science Fiction: Its Nature, Faults and Virtues," Heinlein said that his two sources of information in his creation of "Solution Unsatisfactory" were Campbell and Cornog. But we already know this as a result of the letters that were exchanged between Campbell and Heinlein in early 1940. It is not known precisely how Cornog was involved in the creation of "Solution Unsatisfactory." Did Heinlein ask him for detailed technical assistance or did Cornog review the story before it was submitted, as Heinlein had originally intended with "Blowups Happen"? I think that we may assume that Heinlein kept Cornog aware of the story that he had created.

"Solution Unsatisfactory" appeared in the May 1941 issue of *Astounding*. According to the April 1941 issue, the May issue would be on sale on April 18. With the appearance of "Solution Unsatisfactory" on the newsstands, let us now return to the activities of Ernest Lawrence.

We left Lawrence being notified that he had received the Nobel Prize in Physics in November 1939. The outbreak of war in Europe in September 1939 made it infeasible for Lawrence to make the customary trip to Stockholm. The ceremony was held February 29, 1940 on the Berkeley campus. In Wheeler Hall, Lawrence received his medal from Sweden's consul general in San Francisco.

Although research was being performed at various labs around the country on ^{235}U and details of the fission process, there was no overall direction of such research by the government of the United States. At this point, Leo Szilard re-entered the picture. He convinced Albert Einstein to sign a letter that explained to President Roosevelt the possibility of Nazi Germany developing an atomic bomb. The letter was delivered to the President on October 11, 1939 by one of his advisors, Alexander Sachs.

The immediate result of the letter was the formation of a committee to look at the possible military applications of uranium fission. The director of the National Bureau of Standards, Lyman Briggs, was named chairman. The Army and Navy were represented by Colonel Adamson and Commander Hoover. The first meeting of the committee on October 21 was also attended by a physicist from the Bureau of Standards, another from the Carnegie Institution and three physics consultants: Leo Szilard, Edward Teller and Eugene Wigner.

After what seemed like a fast beginning, the Briggs Committee accomplished very little over the following months. One important change took place in June 1940. The National Defense Research Committee (NDRC) was formed under Vannevar Bush. As the NDRC was to coordinate all research with military applications, it assumed control over the Briggs Committee. Commander Hoover and Colonel Adamson were dropped from the Committee. Additional physicists were added, but any foreign-born scientists were dropped.

Lawrence was only one of the scientists who felt frustrated by the actions of the Briggs Committee. It moved slowly and did not meet often. There was excessive compartmentalization and emphasis on secrecy which prevented access to needed information.

By April 1941, Bush had decided to form a special committee of the National Academy of Sciences to review the work of the Briggs Committee. The president of the Academy, Dr. Frank Jewett, selected the members of the committee: Arthur H. Compton of the University of Chicago, John C. Slater of MIT, John H. van Vleck of Harvard, William D. Coolidge—the retired director of the research lab at General Electric, Bancroft Gherardi—the retired chief engineer of American Telephone and Telegraph and Ernest Lawrence. Gherardi did not serve on the committee because of illness. Coolidge was a chemist; all the others were physicists. The head of the committee was Compton. Its official title was the Advisory Committee of the National Academy on Uranium Disintegration.

The new Committee met with Briggs and other members of his Committee at the Bureau of Standards on April 30. According to Compton, the Briggs Committee seemed to be more concerned with the generation of power than the development of a weapon. The Committee met again on May 5 at Harvard. They continued their discussions and also heard a report from a Harvard physicist, Kenneth Bainbridge, on the state of fission research in Britain. According to the Committee's report, additional conferences were held by mail and wire.

The Advisory Committee submitted their unanimous report on May 17 to Dr. Jewett. There were three proposed military applications:

(a) Production of violently radioactive materials to be used as missiles destructive to life in virtue of their ionizing radiations.

(b) As a power source on submarines and other ships.

(c) Violently explosive bombs.

We shall not be concerned with the rest of the report or subsequent reports submitted in July and November. All we really care about is the first proposed military application – the radioactive materials.

The Allies never considered making use of radioactive material as suggested in the Committee report. There was some concern, however, that the atomic program of Nazi Germany was sufficiently advanced to make use of nuclear reactors to create radioactive materials that could be used in the manner suggested. At the end of the war in Europe, it was discovered that the German atomic program was nowhere near as advanced as had been feared.

So we have radioactive dust in a science fiction story that appeared in mid-April 1941 and the same concept in a National Academy of Sciences report just a month later. That always struck me as a very interesting situation. I want to emphasize that I am not claiming to be the first to point out the close occurrence of these two events. This was done by H. Bruce Franklin and James Gifford.

The question here is, where did the committee get the idea?

The first possibility is that there is no connection between the two events. When I previously wrote about this topic in a paper, I used the term coincidence. A better choice would be parallel thinking. It is perfectly feasible for members of the Advisory Committee to have arrived at the idea of the use of radioactive materials on their own. Perhaps a member of the Committee made the same connection with Carthage that Campbell did. It may be that no such connection with Carthage was necessary. Consider the work done at the Radiation Laboratory and elsewhere with regard to the creation of radioisotopes. It would not take too much of a mental leap to consider a military application for such radioactive materials rather than a medical one.

The second possibility should be obvious, considering what has been discussed in this chapter. Since I have previously mentioned Campbell's "Shhhhh – Don't Mention It!" and Heinlein's "Solution Unsatisfactory," the next possibility is that either the article or the story was the source of the idea.

In this particular case, there is a third possibility to consider. This possibility is Robert Cornog. Through contact with Heinlein, he would have been aware of the story before it appeared in *Astounding*. I can visualize Cornog sitting around with colleagues at Berkeley and saying "This friend of mine wrote a science fiction story where the weapon is radioactive dust." This idea could then have found its way to Lawrence. Of course, this connection of Cornog with the Advisory Committee through Lawrence is pure speculation.

Does there exist any material other than the May 17 report that mentions the dust idea? In his book *Atomic Quest*, Compton discussed the Briggs Committee and said that "Some thought had been given to the possibility of military use of radioactive materials produced by an atomic reactor." In *The New World*, it is stated that Briggs mentioned fission as applied to "radiation bombs" during the April 30 meeting. What is a "radiation bomb"? Is it the same thing that was mentioned by Compton?

Do either of these statements mean the use of dust as proposed in the May 17 report?

What about the Advisory Committee? The May 17 report only mentions the three applications. No information is given regarding the source of each application. I had hoped that the Minutes of the meetings on either April 30 or May 5 would contain such information.

It was possible to obtain the Minutes from the Archives of the National Academy of Sciences. Unfortunately, when the Minutes were examined, they contained no mention of the use of radioactive material, not even as a suggestion from the Briggs Committee. The Minutes of the May 5 meeting referred to reports received from members of the Briggs Committee. As the reports were to be distributed to members of the Advisory Committee, they were not abstracted in the Minutes. It is possible that the answer is contained in one of those reports.

Based on what I have presented above, the possibility does exist that the Briggs Committee was the source of the dust idea. This would eliminate "Solution Unsatisfactory" as the source. I will keep looking to try to find information somewhere that will provide a definite answer. For the moment, however, I will stick with Cornog as the primary connection and "Solution Unsatisfactory" as the next most likely.

Near the end of the Steiner interview with Robert Cornog, he spoke of working on the idea of underwater tankers in the 1950s at Ramo-Wooldridge Corporation. I began to wonder if I would have to go back and modify the Hawthorne chapter. Then at the very end of the interview he said:

> *Well, there were at one time, people who had made tow devices to carry oil which were towed behind ships and then collapsed and put on deck and taken back east. I think it was done in England. It was about this time and that's what put the bug in my ear originally.*

We have a case here where the original story involved a submersible container, but the Dracones developed by Hawthorne were used on the surface. Then we have Cornog apparently becoming aware of what Hawthorne was doing, but his technical comments in the interview were about the advantages of operating such containers underwater.

7

ARE YOU COMFORTABLE?

The problem was a search for comfort.

I will begin the search with a look at the life and some of the works of the science fiction author Robert Anson Heinlein (1907 – 1988). He was born in Butler, Missouri to Rex Ivar and Bam Lyle Heinlein. His birth date was July 7; I wonder if he was ever tempted to play 777 on the lottery? At the end of 1907, the family moved to Kansas City. Robert had two older brothers, Lawrence Lyle and Rex Ivar. He was followed by a sister, Louise, then another brother, Jesse Clare, and two more sisters, Rose Elizabeth and Mary Jean.

As the Heinlein children were growing up, the financial situation of the Heinlein family could best be described as precarious. The father, Rex Ivar, had some health problems. Although he was a hard worker, he was a bit unlucky in business ventures and the choices of companies for whom he worked. Once they were old enough, Robert and his brothers got part-time jobs to help with the finances.

In spite of the time required by such jobs, Robert received good grades in school. He also managed to do a considerable amount of reading that included Mark Twain, Jules Verne, H. G. Wells and Edgar Rice Burroughs. A part-time job in the Kansas City Public Library gave him access to works by Darwin, Plato, Einstein and Freud. He was also exposed to pulp magazines such as *Argosy*, *All-Story* and Hugo Gernsback's *Electrical Experimenter.*.

Robert's older brother, Rex Ivar (sometimes called Ivar to distinguish him from his father), had obtained an appointment to the United States Naval Academy in 1923. The family financial situation would not provide Robert with help for college, so he began to explore the possibility of attending either the Naval Academy or the United States Military Academy.

One means of gaining entry to the Naval Academy is by an appointment by a member of Congress. In 1924-25, there was a limit imposed by the naval appropriations law. The limit was not on the number to be appointed in one year by a member of Congress, but on the number of appointees at the Academy at one time. In 1924, the limit was set to three. This meant a very small plebe class entering in 1924 and one only slightly larger entering in 1925. As a consequence, the Classes of 1928 and 1929 were the smallest in the interwar period.

By exploring all avenues, Heinlein learned that it might be possible to obtain such an appointment from Senator James A. Reed, who was associated with the Pendergast political machine in Kansas City. Heinlein focused his efforts on obtaining the one appointment available from Reed. An application for such an appointment was accompanied by a letter of recommendation. As Heinlein later discovered, there were fifty other applicants for the appointment. While each of the others had supplied a single letter of recommendation, his application was accompanied by fifty letters. In January 1925, he received notification that his appointment to the Naval Academy had come through. In June, he was sworn in as a midshipman in the Class of 1929.

I will not attempt to tell much of his years at Annapolis. As a plebe, he suffered the usual hazing from upperclassman but managed to survive. Every plebe had to participate in one of the Academy's sports. Heinlein was not attracted to any of the body-contact sports such as football or lacrosse. His choice for the required sport was fencing.

Like any midshipman, Heinlein accumulated a number of demerits over his first three years. In addition, his class standing at the beginning of his final year was not exceptional. During that final year, however, he greatly improved his class standing and accumulated no more demerits. He graduated in June 1929 with a class standing of 20 out of 240.

For those interested in knowing more about Heinlein's time at the Naval Academy, I suggest Volume 1 of Bill Patterson's biography of Heinlein.

His first posting following graduation was to the aircraft carrier *Lexington*. Upon returning to Kansas City on the way to San Pedro, California to join his ship, Heinlein married Elinor Curry on June 21, 1929. The marriage can only be called a mistake and was ended by divorce on October 15, 1930.

During the earliest phases of his shipboard career, an ensign such as Heinlein would rotate every three months between areas such as gunnery, engineering and communications. He would also be required to gain an understanding of the various systems of the ship.

In May 1930, Heinlein was detached for temporary duty at the Ford Instrument Company in Long Island City. Ford Instrument (no connection to Ford Motor Co.) manufactured the electromechanical analog computers used in controlling naval gunfire. He found an apartment near Washington Square. Although the training only lasted for six weeks, he quickly became involved with artists and models in Greenwich Village.

When his training was completed and he returned to the *Lexington*, it had a new captain. This was Ernest J. King, who would be both Commander in Chief, United States Fleet and Chief of Naval Operations during World War II.

Under the command of Captain King, the *Lexington* participated in Fleet Problem XII, held in February, 1931. Fleet Problems were naval exercises held during the interwar years. Their purpose of such exercises was to help the navy develop new tactics and to learn the best way to employ new technologies. The Fleet Problems will also be discussed in more detail in Chapter 8.

Fleet Problem XII was held in the Pacific Ocean off Central America and the Panama Canal. The aggressor forces, BLACK, were to seize or destroy the Panama Canal as well as a fictional canal in Nicaragua. To accomplish this, BLACK's forces consisted of most of the Navy's battleships and the carrier *Langley*. The defending force, BLUE, consisted of the battleship *Arkansas*, several cruisers and destroyers, seaplane tender *Wright* and the carriers *Saratoga* and *Lexington*.

In the course of the exercise, four squadrons of planes were sent out from the *Lexington* to attack a portion of the BLACK force heading for the Panama Canal. A pilot in one of the squadrons was Albert "Buddy" Scoles, a close friend of Heinlein from the Class of 1927. Three of the squadrons returned safely in daylight, but Scoles's squadron had navigational problems. Heinlein was aware of the situation as he was on duty in Communications.

As night approached, the squadron would have difficulty in locating the *Lexington*. The pilots would also be required to make night landings, a rare thing at that time. Captain King cancelled radio silence and ordered the ships to turn on all searchlights. With these aids, all of the planes were able to locate the *Lexington* and land safely. The last plane to land was the one piloted by Buddy Scoles.

Following the Fleet Problem, Heinlein was temporarily detached from the *Lexington* and sent to Fort Clayton, located in the Panama Canal Zone. The purpose was for him to compete in the Fleet rifle and pistol matches. After taps, having returned from Panama City, he would go over to the large swimming pool on the base. There was no one else present, so he would strip down and float in the pool. Heinlein said that he was one of those people who could not sink, even in fresh water. He would just float there and relax, possibly dozing off for a while, and then climb out and return to his tent. The importance of this story will soon become apparent.

On the *Lexington*, life went on during 1931. Heinlein had stayed in contact with Caleb Barrett Laning, a classmate and close friend. Laning had a new girl, Leslyn MacDonald. Laning was seriously thinking of proposing marriage. When Heinlein met her in January 1932, he was even more impressed with her. He spent the night with her and proposed to her the next morning. Leslyn was somewhat surprised but accepted. Matters then moved quickly to a wedding on March 28. This marriage lasted longer than his first but ended in divorce in 1947.

The month of June 1932 meant even more changes in Heinlein's life. With others in the Class of 1929, Heinlein had taken the necessary examinations for promotion to lieutenant. On June 6, three years after becoming an ensign, he was promoted to lieutenant junior grade. On June 10, Ernest King was relieved as Captain of the *Lexington*.

One of King's acts before leaving the *Lexington* was to recommend that Heinlein be retained on board as gunnery officer. This made sense, since his training at the Ford Instrument Company and subsequent shipboard experience meant that he knew quite a lot about the operation of the electromechanical computers used for fire control. Unfortunately, the Navy did not act on King's recommendation and Heinlein was ordered on June 20 to report to the destroyer *Roper*.

Service on the *Roper* was detrimental to Heinlein's health. Unlike the large and stable *Lexington*, the *Roper* bounced and rolled so much when at sea that he was always seasick. No effective remedies existed at the time, so he continued to lose weight. In an emaciated condition, he went to the U.S. Naval Hospital in San Diego in December 1932. During the course of the examination, it was discovered that he had contracted pulmonary tuberculosis. It is possible that the bacterium was already in his system, and only became active when his system was weakened by seasickness.

This was before the existence of antibiotics that could treat tuberculosis (TB). All the doctors could do was to hope for a spontaneous cure. Heinlein's brother Ivar had also developed TB and was being treated at Fitzsimmons Army Hospital near Denver, which handled all TB cases for the armed services. Heinlein was able to gain permission to go on leave to be initially treated at the Pottinger Clinic in Monrovia, California.

At the expiration of his extended leave, he was ordered to the Fitzsimmons Hospital. He did not do well with the care received there, both with regard to the TB and other medical problems. One of his recollections from this time was:

> Some years later, bothered by bed sores and with every joint aching no matter what position I twisted into, I thought often of the Sybaritic comfort of floating in blood-warm water at night in Panama—and wished that it could be done for bed patients . . . and eventually figured out how to do it, all details, long before I was well enough to make working drawings.

He had disputes with the doctors at Fitzsimmons and only succeeded in getting a serious bladder problem treated properly by going to an outside specialist. Gradually, his health began to improve. It was during this time that he met Robert Cornog (see Chapter 6). Unfortunately, his physical condition was such that he realized that he would soon be retired from the Navy. The medical retirement process began in March 1934 and the decision was made to retire him as "totally and permanently disabled" as of August 1, 1934. This meant that he would receive retirement pay of two-thirds of his full service pay as a lieutenant junior grade.

Following his retirement, Robert and Leslyn lived in California. He tried to go for a graduate degree, but was handicapped by the fact that when he had graduated from the Naval Academy it did not issue bachelor's degrees. Over the following years, he became very involved in California politics. In 1938, he ran in the Democratic primary for State Assemblyman but was defeated.

In the spring of 1939, Heinlein wrote a 7,000-word short story "Life-Line" and sent it to John W. Campbell, Jr., the editor of *Astounding Science-Fiction*. Campbell bought the story at the prevailing rate of one cent a word. This meant a payment of $70.00. That may not seem like much now, but consider some of the prices in 1939: milk, 15 cents a quart; eggs, 25 cents a dozen; a loaf of bread, 7 cents. When Heinlein received the check, he said:

> How long has this racket been going on? And why didn't anybody tell me about it sooner?

And thus began a career that lasted almost 50 years until his death in 1988. The one gap in that career was for his work as a civilian engineer at the Naval Aircraft Factory in Philadelphia during World War II. It is a career that gave birth to many short stories and novels and resulted in many awards for Heinlein, including four Hugo Awards for Best Novel. I was introduced to Heinlein by reading *Space Cadet* when I was in the third grade, and he remains my favorite science fiction author.

Heinlein never took his ideas for a comfortable hospital bed beyond the planning stages. He did, however, include variations of the idea in several of his stories. Of all of his published works, they are the only ones that we will look at here.

We first encounter the waterbed in *Beyond This Horizon*. This was Heinlein's first novel-length published work and appeared in the April and May 1942 issues of *Astounding Science-Fiction* as by Anson MacDonald. It is the story of a future society that turns out not to be quite the utopia as first presented. The story has been noted for setting the story in the future with a simple phrase on the first page: "the door dilated." At the beginning of the second chapter, the principal character Hamilton Felix has returned home and gets ready to go to bed:

> The water rose gently under the skin of the mattress until he floated, dry and warm and snug. . . . Hamilton became aware that the water had drained out of his bed, and that he lay with nothing between him and the spongy bottom but the sheet and the waterproof skin.

In the August 1942 issue of *Astounding*, there appeared the novella "Waldo," also as by Anson MacDonald. The titular character, Waldo, suffers from childhood from a muscle weakness described as "not entirely *myasthenia gravis*." His inventive mind, aided by his family's wealth, enable him to develop means of coping with his condition:

> The deceleration tanks which are now standard equipment for the lunar mail ships traced their parentage to a flotation tank in which Waldo habitually had eaten and slept up to the point when he left the home of his parents for his present, somewhat unique, home.

The unique home to which the quote refers is an orbiting space station where Waldo lives and moves in conditions of zero-g. He develops and uses remote manipulators that are capable of greatly multiplying the actions of his feeble muscles. These manipulators were called "waldoes" in the story. When remote manipulators were developed to handle intensely radioactive materials during the Manhattan Project, they were sometimes called "waldos." Waldo decides to make a trip back to earth, so must again make use of a means of cushioning himself against gravity and acceleration:

The tank was not a standard deceleration type, but a modification built for this one trip. The tank was roughly the shape of an oversized coffin. and was swung in gymbals to keep it always normal to the axis of absolute acceleration. Waldo floated in water — the specific gravity of his fat hulk was low — from which he was separated by the usual flexible, gasketed tarpaulin. Supporting his head and shoulders was a pad shaped to his contour. A mechanical artificial resuscitator was built into the tank, the back pads being under water, the breast pads out of the water but retracted out of the way.

We next encounter the waterbed, again in its use as an acceleration tank, in the short story "Sky Lift," which originally appeared in the November 1953 issue of *Imagination*. It is the story of a trip to deliver emergency medical supplies to a base located on Pluto. The problem is that the time constraint requires that the trip be made with sustained acceleration at high g-levels. The two men of the crew had to be properly cushioned to have any chance of survival:

Each tank was like an oversized bathtub filled with a liquid denser than water. The top was covered by a rubbery sheet, gasketed at the edges; during boost each man would float with the sheet conforming to his body.

The final appearance of the waterbed as a means of coping with high acceleration was in the novel *Double Star*. A story of interplanetary intrigue and the impersonation of a key political figure, it appeared in *Astounding* from February thru April 1956. The actor who has agreed to perform the impersonation must be transported quickly to Mars, so we have:

Against one bulkhead and flat to it were two bunks, or "cider presses," the bathtub-shaped, hydraulic, pressure-distribution tanks used for high acceleration in torchships.

In *Stranger in a Strange Land*, published in 1961, we come across the waterbed in the sense it which it was originally conceived by Heinlein: a hospital bed. *Stranger* is the story of Valentine Michael Smith. He was born on Mars to survivors of the first expedition and then raised by the Martians. Twenty-five years later, the second expedition found him and brought him to earth, where he was held incommunicado by the government in a hospital. It is here we encounter multiple references to a water bed:

. . . transferred into a hydraulic bed.

The patient floated in the flexible skin of the hydraulic bed.

"Sure, you're weak as a kitten but you'll never put on muscle floating in that bed." Nelson opened a valve, water drained out. . . . Shortly he lay on the floor of the bed with the watertight cover wrinkled around him. . . . "Here, help me lift him into bed. No— fill it first." Frame cut off the flow when the skin floated six inches from the top.

He switched on the Peeping Tom above his desk; Jill saw in it a water bed; floating in it was a tiny old woman.

He went to a hydraulic bed in the center of the room. . . . Floating, half concealed by the way his body sank into the plastic skin and covered to his armpits by a sheet, was a young man.

A patient that old can smother in a water bed.

Note that in *Beyond This Horizon* and *Stranger in a Strange Land*, Heinlein has the waterbed being filled and emptied, as opposed to our normal practice of keeping it filled.

If you search online, there are several references to the history of the waterbed. The problem is sorting things out. There is the story of the Persians using water-filled goatskins for beds thousands of years ago. The origin of that particular story is not known. It is when we get to the nineteenth century that we begin to see many references to the waterbed. We first encounter Dr. Arnott and then Dr. William Hooper.

Dr. Neil Arnott was a Scottish physician and inventor. He received the Rumford medal for his development of a smokeless grate, also known as "Arnott's stove." Here we will be concerned with another of his inventions, the waterbed. Unlike many other references to historical waterbeds, it was possible to find a description of Arnott's design.

In an issue of *The London Medical and Surgical Journal* from 1833, the text of a lecture by a Professor Cooper is presented in which he describes Arnott's *hydrostatic bed*:

... it consists of a kind of trough, capable of holding water to the depth of about six inches, which is covered with a cloth, rendered water-proof with a coating of elastic gum or some other sort of varnish. By lying on a bed constructed on this principle, the patient floats on water without touching it.

In *An Encyclopædia of Domestic Economy* (1855), a discussion of Dr. Arnott's bed identifies a major design problem in that the cloth, however treated, will decay in from six months to a year. The discussion closes by suggesting that this problem could be avoided by a "material of superior manufacture."

Many online references to Dr. Hooper state that he patented his waterbed, with various dates given for the patent. The biggest problem we have is that Hooper was not a doctor. According to his obituary, which appeared in the October 15, 1878 issue of *The Telegraphic Journal and Electrical Review*, he was a pharmaceutical chemist. The notice of his death appeared in such a publication since he was also known as the inventor and manufacturer of india-rubber insulated wire. With regard to other products involving india-rubber, the obituary also states he was known:

as the inventor and manufacturer of water beds, &c., for invalids, which at one time were in use in over 1,000 hospitals and similar institutions.

It has not been possible to find any description of Hooper's waterbed or whether he ever actually obtained a patent for it.

One may also find literary references to the waterbed. It is mentioned multiple times in Elizabeth Gaskell's 1853 novel *North and South*. Mark Twain referred to waterbeds in an article published in *The New York Times* in 1871. H. G. Wells used the waterbed in his 1899 novel *When the Sleeper Wakes* (and in the 1910 revision *The Sleeper Awakes*). I find it interesting that all of these authors simply employed the term with no explanation or description, as if expecting the reader to know what was meant.

We now come to the year 1968 and the invention of the modern waterbed. The inventor was Charles Prior Hall (1943 –). In every article on the waterbed that I have found, the story begins with Hall as a 24-year-old graduate student who has just invented the waterbed. It is as if someone had waved a magic wand and both the inventor and his invention have miraculously appeared in a cloud of smoke. Here I will attempt to provide a bit of his background and what led him to invent the waterbed.

Charlie Hall was born in Miami Beach, Florida. As a child, he liked discovering how things work and taking things apart. It is not known how successful he was in putting such things back together.

Hall went to school in Miami Beach until he went to St. Louis to attend a boarding college prep school. When he came home, he entered the University of Miami as a business major in the fall of 1962. This choice of major was probably due to a parental suggestion.

His first two years at college were not unhappy, but he did not consider it a very exciting life. He was living at home and commuting to campus. Some of his friends from the prep school were from California and suggested that he should move to California to complete his college degree.

In the fall of 1964, Hall was a student at San Francisco State College (renamed San Francisco State University in 1974). He chose San Francisco because of its interesting culture and creativity. Starting as a business major, he then made several changes. He drifted to political science, then art, then photography, and finally history. He received his B.A. in history in 1967.

One day on campus, Hall saw an exhibit that had been sponsored by the Department of Design and Industry. He decided to enter that department for his M.A. The department then had a program called Design, Art, Industry (DAI) that allowed you to build a degree from many disciplines.

The faculty member for whom Hall did his master's project was James Baldwin. This James Baldwin was an industrial designer who was a student of Buckminster Fuller. He received his undergraduate degree from the University of Michigan and did graduate work at the University of California, Berkeley. Aside from San Francisco State College, Baldwin also taught at several other California colleges, simultaneously in some cases. From 1968 to 1998, he was the co-editor with Stewart Brand of the *Whole Earth Catalog*.

According to Hall:

He really stretched my mind to look at things in unconventional ways and allowed enough freedom to explore ideas outside the box.

The students in Baldwin's class were allowed to choose a problem to be solved for their project. Hall came up with the problem of making furniture more comfortable.

As part of the research for this chapter, I attempted to get hold of his master's thesis from the SFSU Library. I was informed that certain master's programs provide the option to the students of doing "field study" or "creative work." A thesis based on such work would not be in the Library's collection, being retained instead by the appropriate department. Hall's thesis was placed in the files of the Department and Design and Industry. The department policy was to let students check out the old theses for reference purposes. Apparently, someone checked out Hall's thesis and never returned it. To his recollection, the title of his thesis was "Liquid Support for Human Bodies."

Hall began his project as a historian and performed a review of furniture design. This review covered designers such as Marcel Brueur, Florence Knoll, Charles and Ray Eames and Mies van der Rohe. One thing that it showed him was that much design was focused on style and the sculptural aspects rather than a consideration of comfort. Anyone who has had to sit for some time in a fancy but uncomfortable chair can agree with that result.

He then focused on the concept of floating. As he described it:

Floating is a very primal sensation. You have to be relaxed to float; you are relaxed when you float. Physical therapists, psychiatrists, doctors; all seem to agree on that. Temperature was a very important element to achieve a relaxed state. The elimination of pressure points was a key objective to avoid discomfort and a lack of circulation which causes people to move or shift their weight to restore blood flow to an area of the body.

You should compare this with Heinlein's statement on the discomfort he suffered while in the hospital.

Hall began with the design for a comfortable chair. He said that "Every furniture designer seems to produce their signature chair." In his first attempt, he took a large inflatable bag and filled it with 300 pounds of a liquid cornstarch mixture. In addition to the weight, this design had certain disadvantages. It was very hard to get in and out of the chair and it felt cold and clammy when you were in it. After a period of time, the cornstarch mixture began to smell. A second chair experiment replaced the cornstarch with Jell-O. It was no more successful than the first attempt.

He then turned to the idea of a bed. Before anyone asks, Hall says that he was not aware of the works of Heinlein until after he developed the waterbed.

The first question was, what should be used to fill the bed? Neither of the chair experiments were full-scale. For a bed, cost considerations prohibited the use of either material used to fill the chairs. Another consideration was temperature control. He realized that if any kind of viscous material had been employed to fill the bed, a very large heater would have been required. Even then there could have been an uneven distribution of temperature. The only material that would satisfy these problems was plain water.

The waterbed was constructed at Hall's residence at 131 Octavia Street. This is just off Haight Street about 10 blocks east of the Haight-Ashbury district. But well within the influence of the hippie culture of the time, including the Summer of Love in 1967.

His residence was in an old pre-earthquake townhouse. Hall was on the second floor. When I asked him about the weight issue of the waterbed, he said:

> From the street, the house seems to list a bit to the right. I think after I filled my waterbed, it may actually have straightened the place up a bit. Anyway, that's my theory.

In any case, the old floor stood up under the load.

The location presented a problem when his project was completed. The normal process would be for a student to bring his or her project to the school for evaluation. This was clearly not possible with the waterbed. It was necessary for people to travel from the campus, a trip of about 5 miles, to see the waterbed.

The waterbed was eventually displayed at the Cannery Gallery in San Francisco.

What were the features of the waterbed as designed by Charlie Hall? To get an answer, we must take a look at his patent. The application was filed on July 27, 1970 and granted on June 15, 1971. This was patent 3,585,356 "Liquid Support for Human Bodies." For those with an interest in viewing the patent, a link is provided by the Wikipedia page for the Waterbed. This link takes you to the page on https://patents.google.com from which a PDF file of the patent may be downloaded.

First consider the general description as stated in the patent's Abstract:

> An article of furniture comprising a flexible bladder which is substantially filled with a liquid. A supporting framework is provided for holding the liquid filled bladder in such manner that a body resting upon the bladder is floatably supported by the liquid. Heating means is provided for maintaining a temperature of the liquid at a temperature on the order of the Temperature of the human body. In some embodiments, solid particles, such as styrofoam, are disposed in the bladder to dampen shock waves in

the liquid and to provide additional support for a body resting upon the bladder.

The Abstract, and the patent as a whole, was written so as to not restrict the scope to items simply filled with water. Although the use of water is mentioned at several points, most of the text makes use of either "liquid" or "fluid."

The body of the patent contains a Background of the Invention, Summary and Objects of the Invention, Brief Description of the Drawings (there are 11) and a Description of Preferred Embodiments. This last section concludes with a listing of the Claims of the patent. I will defer a discussion of the Claims until a bit later in the chapter.

In the Summary section, deficiencies of previous support systems were noted. The first was the tendency of water to react to pressure by the creation of a shock wave. The second was the clammy feeling experienced by the user if the fluid is not heated.

These problems were addressed in the Embodiments section. One solution to the shock wave problem was to place grease, gelatin or other highly viscous material within the bag. This suggestion was made in spite of the problems encountered with the use of similar viscous materials in the chairs. Another proposed solution was the addition of Styrofoam, either as small pieces dispersed throughout the water or as a layer of small blocks that would cover the entire surface of the water to provide additional support for the body. The solution of the second problem was by the introduction of a heating element and a suitably mounted thermostat.

This patent was assigned to Innerspace Environments, Inc., which was the first company formed by Hall. Innerspace was based in San Francisco. This company failed, according to Hall, because of high overhead, expensive locations and a huge advertising budget.

His next company was Basic Designs, Inc., based in Sausalito. The company was focused on outdoor products for camping and boating. One such product was The Sun Shower, which consisted of a bag formed of a clear plastic sheet bonded with a black plastic sheet. By filling the bag with water and hanging it so that the clear face was towards the sun, the water would be heated to a temperature suitable for a shower, using a hose and shower head attached to the bottom of the bag. Basic Designs was a profitable business that was sold to a division of K2, Inc. and by them to the Coleman Company, Inc.

Hall's third business was Advanced Elements, in which his partner is another SFSU alumnus. This is Clay Haller, who has a B.A. in Industrial Design from 1995. Haller was also associated with Hall at Basic Designs.

Advanced Elements is based in Benicia, a town in the North Bay region of the San Francisco Bay area. It manufactures inflatable kayaks, inflatable stand-up paddleboards and accessories.

By my count, Hall has almost 40 patents to his name. A large number of these were concerned with improvements to the waterbed. Nine patents proposed different types of baffle structures internal to the waterbed to reduce the wave action. These were intended to improve on the suggestions made in the original patent.

Now let us return to Robert Heinlein.

I first encountered Heinlein's connection with the waterbed when I read his book *Expanded Universe*. This collection of short stories and essays, along with extensive commentary material by Heinlein, was published in 1980. Heinlein began the essay "The Happy Days Ahead" by pointing out the problems of making predictions. As example of one of his successful predictions, he pointed to the waterbed.

There are three quotes from the essay that must be presented here and analyzed in turn. In the first quote we have:

> Some joker tried to patent the water bed to shut out competition and discovered that he could not do so because it was in the public domain, having been described in detail in STRANGER IN A STRANGE LAND. It had been mentioned in stories of mine as far back as 1941 and several times after that. But not until STRANGER did the mechanics of a scene require describing how it worked.

Was Charlie Hall the "joker" to whom Heinlein referred? If so, then we know that Heinlein was in error, as Hall was able to obtain his patent. Or was he referring to someone else? How does the appearance of a concept in a story prevent a patent from being issued? That question will be addressed in a bit.

Heinlein said that the waterbed was described in detail in *Stranger*. Let us first look at the description in *Beyond This Horizon*, which was published in 1942 but written in 1941. There is a waterproof skin and a means for filling and draining. A means of heating is not mentioned, although Hamilton Felix is described as being "warm and snug."

As I see it, the description obtained from all of the quotes taken from *Stranger* actually provide less information than *Beyond This Horizon*. The bed employs a flexible plastic skin and a means to drain or fill the bed. No mention is made of temperature control. Please note that this refers to the version of *Stranger* published in 1961 and not the uncut version published years later

The second quote describes how Heinlein acquired his own waterbed:

It was not the first man to build water beds who tried to patent it. The first man in the field knew where it came from; he sent me one, free and freight prepaid, with a telegram naming his firm as the "Share-Water Bed Company.

This quote is backed up with additional information from Volume 2 of Bill Patterson's biography of Heinlein. In August 1970, Heinlein received the waterbed accompanied by a letter, not a telegram, from Timothy Hamilton of Share-Water Bed. According to Heinlein, this company was located in Hollywood. Heinlein was unable to make use of the waterbed as the floor of his house could not stand the load of a ton of water within the footprint of the waterbed. Unfortunately, I have been unable to locate additional information on Mr. Hamilton or his company. It is not possible for me to say whether or not he was actually the "first man in the field."

The third quote allows me to bring together a number of points. Earlier I said that I would discuss the Claims contained in the original waterbed patent. I also said that I would discuss Heinlein's comment that the idea was in the public domain as a consequence of it being described in a story.

The third quote from the essay is as follows:

I designed the water bed during years as a bed patient in the middle thirties: a pump to control water-level, side supports to permit one to float rather than simply lying on a not-very-soft water-filled mattress, thermostatic control of temperature, safety interfaces to avoid all possibility of electrical shock, waterproof box to make a leak no more important than a leaky hot water bottle rather than a domestic disaster, calculation of floor loads (important!), internal rubber mattress, and lighting, reading and eating arrangements - an attempt to design the perfect hospital bed by one who had spent too *damned* much time in hospital beds.

The essay containing this quote was written in 1979, several years after the waterbed patent was issued. The quote taken from "The Happy Days Ahead" contains many details of the waterbed as envisioned by Heinlein: pump, side supports, temperature control. It was probably useful for him to have such a picture in his mind, but he did not include all of that detail in any of his stories.

According to the United States Code, there are four conditions that must be satisfied to permit the granting of a patent. The idea must (1) Be of patentable subject matter, (2) Be Novel, (3) Be Non-Obvious and (4) Be Useful.

Here we are concerned with the second condition, that of Novelty. If we look at Title 35 of United States Code, section 102, as it existed at that time, we find:

A person shall be entitled to a patent unless –

(a) the invention was known or used by others in this country, or patented or described in a printed publication in this or a foreign country, before the invention thereof by the applicant for patent, or

(b) the invention was patented or described in a printed publication in this or a foreign country or in public use or on sale in this country, more than one year prior to the date of the application for patent in the United States, or . . .

There are additional conditions in the Code regarding Novelty, but they are not relevant to us here. From a reading of the law, and with the knowledge that the waterbed was featured in stories published years before the application was made for the patent by Hall, how was he able to obtain the patent?

It comes down to a question of how much detail is provided in the publication. In a technical publication, it is possible for a great deal of information to be conveyed about some device or system. But what about a work of fiction? In cases such as the transporter or warp drive from *Star Trek* or the flux capacitor from *Back to the Future*, I don't think we have to worry much about someone filing an application for a patent anytime soon.

What about those stories where it seems that it might be possible to construct the fictional device? The author of such a story is not interested in promoting the device; he or she is simply telling a story.

Is it possible for works of fiction to provide sufficient information to prevent someone from obtaining a patent? The best example is related to a ship capsizing in the harbor of Kuwait in 1964. The ship was carrying several thousand sheep. The ship had to be raised as quickly as possible before their carcasses started decomposing and causing pollution. Conventional methods with cranes would have taken too long. A Danish inventor named Karl Krøyer came up with a solution to fill the ship with buoyant objects. He had 27,000,000 balls made of expandable polystyrene foam shipped to Kuwait where they were pumped into the ship. These balls displaced the water and up came the ship.

Krøyer, as would be expected, tried to obtain a patent in various countries. This is where the details become a bit vague. He was successful in the United Kingdom and Germany but was supposedly refused in the Netherlands. Someone had discovered a 1949 issue of a Donald Duck comic book with a story called "The Sunken Yacht." One picture shows Donald's nephews feeding ping pong balls down a tube. The next picture shows the tube feeding into the hull of the sunken ship. It is clearly the same technique that Krøyer was trying to patent. Any patent office that had been aware of the comic book would have rejected the patent as showing that the idea was not novel.

In general, how does one evaluate the amount of information provided? Here we have the concept of a "person having ordinary skill in the art" (PHOSITA). To prevent the issuing of a patent, the information provided in the publication must enable a PHOSITA to make the invention, with the additional condition that it must be done without undue experimentation. Conversely, if a person obtains only vague or limited information from the publication and has to do much development work to bring the idea to completion, a patent might be possible.

So where does that leave us with regard to the waterbed? Someone reading Heinlein's stories could clearly have been inspired to create a type of waterbed. But how would such an invention compare with what was claimed in Hall's patent? For this we must take a look at the Claims taken from patent 3,585,356. The language of the Claims section is extremely structured and repetitive. To save space and to avoid frustrating the reader, I have simplified what was said. The claims include:

- Support for floatably supporting a plurality of adult human bodies
- A bladder formed of substantially inelastic material
- Bladder defining a single closed chamber
- Body of liquid enclosed within and filling bladder so that there is substantially no air in bladder
- A rigid framework providing lateral support for the body of liquid in bladder and preventing lateral distortion
- Means of supporting bottom of bladder to confine within framework
- Body of liquid and upper wall support human bodies on the upper surface such that contours of bodies are accommodated and there is no contact with bottom wall of bladder

- A means of heating the body of liquid to maintain at a desired temperature
- Particles of solid matter disposed within bladder to dampen shock waves to minimize disturbance to one body by movement of others

I would ask the reader to compare these claims with the quotes from Heinlein's stories. What is included in the patent but not described in the stories consists of (1) the rigid framework for support and to prevent distortion, (2) the need to prevent contact of the supported body and upper wall with the lower wall of the bladder and finally, what I consider the most important, (3) the inclusion of solid material within the bladder to dampen shock waves. With regard to (2), the waterbeds in *Beyond This Horizon* and *Stranger* were specifically operated so that the bed would be drained, bringing the supported body and upper wall into contact with the lower wall of the bladder.

I am not a patent attorney or a patent examiner. All of my knowledge on the subject has been obtained from the available literature. However, it seems to me that even if the patent examiners were aware of the stories of Robert Heinlein, there exist claims that were made by Hall that have no counterpart in those stories. I conclude that the waterbed as described by Hall was novel and that there should not have been any problem in obtaining the patent. To the best of my knowledge, no one has ever tried to have the patent invalidated because it was not novel.

Both Heinlein and Hall were inspired by floating. In Heinlein's case, it was from his desire to recreate the comfort experienced when floating in the pool at Fort Clayton. In Hall's case, it was from a careful study of the problem of comfort for his project. With the same inspiration, we should not be surprised that they independently developed very similar designs for the waterbed.

This is not the end of the story of Charlie Hall or the waterbed. Charlie Hall has introduced a new version of the waterbed. In conjunction with Keith Koenig and Michael Geraghty, Hall has formed Hall Flotation in Tamarac, Florida. Koenig is the CEO of City Furniture, a South Florida furniture chain formerly known as Waterbed City. Geraghty is a former waterbed manufacturer. The new waterbed carries the name AFLOAT and the slogan "Not your parents' waterbed." The waterbed premiered in June 2018 at a number of City Furniture stores.

A picture of Charlie Hall on one of his new AFLOAT waterbeds is shown in Figure 11. What is different about AFLOAT? As he described it to me:

I tried to expand on all the positive aspects of the waterbed and eliminate some of the negatives. Features will include: improved motion suppression, greater conforming surface for reduced pressure points, slightly lighter weight, individual temperature controls for right and left sides of the bed. Easier to get in and out of.

Will Charlie Hall succeed in the introduction of a new waterbed to a new generation, fifty years after the creation of the original?

Figure 11. Charlie Hall relaxing on one of his new AFLOAT waterbeds. (Photo courtesy of C. Hall.)

8

WHERE IS THE ENEMY?

The problem was the management of a naval battle.

Let us begin with a look at naval warfare in the days of sail. The ships were capable of moving at what we would consider a low speed, perhaps 10 to 15 knots under the best conditions, usually more like five to eight knots. The guns were muzzle loaders capable of firing at a range of between one and two miles. The captain of such a ship was not troubled by the possibility of attack from beneath the sea or from the sky. All he had to do was cope with the ships that he could see with the naked eye or with his spyglass. A slight increase in the range of observation was possible by information passed from the seamen stationed in the crow's nest at the top of the mainmast. Any ship that he could not see was not likely to be an immediate problem.

As the ships were powered by the wind, it was also necessary to consider the weather gauge. The ship that was upwind of its opponent was able to maneuver as it wished and then bring either broadside into action. The ship that was downwind was restricted in its movements and in the use of its guns. The general situation was that the captain walking the quarterdeck was quite capable of coping with the information about a pending or ongoing battle that he could personally gather.

This all begin to change during the nineteenth century. The most obvious changes were the replacement of sail by steam propulsion and the construction of ships from iron instead of wood. Guns became more powerful, changing from muzzle-loaders to breech-loaders that fired explosive shells instead of solid shot. They became capable of hurling those shells at greater and greater ranges. The elimination of the weather gauge meant that a ship could attack or be attacked from any direction.

By the early days of the twentieth century, other technologies entered into the problem of fighting a naval battle. The development of the submarine and the airplane meant there were additional threats and threat directions to consider. There was also radio, which provided the ability to communicate over much greater ranges than possible with signal flags or blinkers. All of these changes made battles more complex and faster moving. The captain could no longer base his decisions solely on what he could see from the bridge of his destroyer, cruiser or battleship.

One of the answers to the captain's problems was another new technology, but with this new technology came the question of how it could be used to its greatest benefit.

Let us begin by considering one of the previously mentioned technologies – radio. It began with the equations developed by Scottish mathematician and physicist James Clerk Maxwell (1831 – 1879). These showed that an electromagnetic wave will propagate at the speed of light. What we call visible light is composed of electromagnetic waves over a particular band of frequencies. Only nine years after Maxwell's death, Heinrich Hertz (1857 – 1894) was able to show that electromagnetic waves could be generated at frequencies many orders of magnitude lower than visible light. These waves were in the range of 31 to 1250 MHz.

It was Guglielmo Marconi (1874 – 1937) who took Hertz's laboratory work and extended the range to the point where it had practical applications. Messages were sent using Morse code, as it took many years for the techniques of voice transmission to be developed. In 1896, Marconi was able to transmit three miles. By 1901, he was able to transmit across the Atlantic, from Poldhu, Cornwall to St. John's, Newfoundland.

As early as 1901, there was interest on the part of the United States Navy (as well as the Navies of other nations) in radio communication. The technology as demonstrated by Marconi was primitive and presented problems in its use for naval communications. During the years that followed, new technologies were introduced that made it possible for the Navy to communicate between shore stations and all type of naval craft and eventually aircraft.

The means of generating the radio waves used by Marconi was the spark gap. A voltage is increased in a circuit until it jumps the spark gap. The spark gap is connected to a resonant circuit and an antenna. The energy introduced into the resonant circuit resulted in high frequency oscillations that caused electromagnetic waves to be sent out from the antenna. As the waves were transmitted, the oscillations in the resonant circuit would rapidly die out. Instead of a single frequency, this process generated a collection of radio frequencies. The means of forcing most of the energy to appear at one frequency was accomplished by the design of the antenna. One of the greatest advances in the early days of radio was the development of a system for tuning.

If the damped oscillations from a spark gap system could be replaced with a continuous wave, it would be possible to transmit only at a desired frequency. One approach was the Poulsen arc transmitter, based on the arc lamp. Unlike the spark gap, the electrical discharge between the electrodes in an arc is continuous. By connecting a series resonant circuit between the two electrodes, a continuous signal would be generated. It was Valdemar Poulsen (1869 – 1942) who found a way to make the system operate at useful radio frequencies.

Another approach to the generation of continuous waves was similar to the means of generating the AC power that we use everywhere. The frequency of AC power in most locations is either 50 or 60 Hz. Ernst Alexanderson (1878 – 1975) developed an alternator capable of operating at higher frequencies, up to 100 kHz. This approach generated continuous waves at a single frequency, ideal for radio transmission. There were, however, problems preventing its use for all applications. The first was that the frequency was determined by the speed of rotation of the alternator, which placed an upper limit on the frequency that could be generated. The second was the size of the alternator. For naval applications, it could be used at ground stations, but was too large to install on most ships.

The ultimate solution was the vacuum tube. This was the basis of all electronic systems until it was replaced by the transistor following World War II. There are still applications, however, where vacuum tubes are employed. The vacuum tube grew out of early experiments done with incandescent light bulbs. A plate was placed inside the bulb along with the filament and an external connection provided to the plate. It was found that an electric current was flowing from the filament to the plate.

That is where matters stood until Professor John Fleming hooked a battery between the filament and the plate. If the battery was connected such that the plate was positive with respect to the filament, a current flowed. If the battery was reversed so that the plate was negative with respect to the filament, no current flowed. Any electrons emitted from the filament would be attracted by a positive plate but repelled by a negative plate. This process converts an alternating current signal to a signal that flows in only one direction. This has many applications in electronics, but was not the solution to the problem of generating continuous waves. In many tubes, the filament is used to heat a terminal called the cathode but is not connected to it electrically. The plate is sometimes called the anode. The current flow is then from the cathode to the anode.

The answer came in 1906 when Lee De Forest placed a third element called the grid between the anode and the cathode. With the anode positive with respect to the cathode, a current will flow as in the simpler device. By varying the voltage on the grid, it was then possible to control the current flowing between cathode and anode. In a properly designed circuit, a small voltage variation in the input controls the grid, which causes a larger voltage variation in the output circuit containing the anode. This process is called amplification. It was no longer necessary to be content with the weak signal that was picked up by your antenna. Amplification of the received signal made communication possible over larger ranges.

Amplification could be enhanced by feeding back part of the output signal to the input. It was then discovered that if the feedback was increased, the circuit would begin to oscillate at some frequency. This was bad if you wanted to amplify a signal, but was perfect for the generation of continuous waves. If the feedback path includes a resonant circuit of some type, it is easy to generate any desirable frequency by selecting circuit components of the proper values. This was the answer to the transmitter problem.

The basic tube with three elements (cathode, grid and anode) was logically called a triode. Even when the triode was made more reliable, the basic design had some limitations. It was found that performance could be improved by the addition of another grid between the original control grid and the anode. When this grid, called the screen grid, was held at a slight positive potential, it had two effects. It screened the grid from the effects of a large anode voltage and also helped to accelerate the electrons towards the anode. Since the tube had four elements, it was called a tetrode. The next major change was the additional of another grid, located between the screen grid and the anode, to create the pentode. This grid was held at the same voltage as the cathode. The main flow of electrons to the anode could cause additional electrons to be knocked loose. The suppressor grid kept these electrons from reaching the screen grid.

I would be willing to bet that many of the readers of this chapter have never even seen a vacuum tube.

As the Navy began to use radios, it began with spark gaps, then made use of arcs, then alternators and finally the vacuum tube. The interest of the Navy in the vacuum tube had a very important effect. Just before World War I, the Bureau of Steam Engineering put out a requisition for tubes with a life of 5,000 hours and a cost of 10 dollars. Western Electric said that they could meet the requirements, but suggested that a better approach was a tube with a life of 2,000 hours and a cost of only $4.50. The Navy knew a good deal when they saw it and modified the requisition.

Not only did the Navy get the tubes they desired, but tubes would soon become available to the public at a reasonable price.

In 1923, the radio operations of the Bureau of Engineering (formerly the Bureau of Steam Engineering) were transferred to the newly created Naval Research Laboratory (NRL). The NRL was then responsible for improving the radio communications of the United States Navy. I will not go into a detailed presentation of the activities of the NRL and will only mention it as needed. For those with an interest in its activities and accomplishments, I can suggest *Evolution of Naval Radio Electronics and Contributions of the Naval Research Laboratory* by Louis A. Gebhard.

So far, I have only discussed the hardware. Another important question was how the hardware should be employed. You don't just put a radio on a ship and that's all there is to it.

One problem was personnel. There had to be men on board the ship capable of keeping the radios operating properly, which in the early days was a real challenge. Particularly in the early days, everything was sent by Morse code. You just didn't pick up a microphone and talk to someone else. The operators had to be capable of sending code accurately and at a reasonable speed. More important, they had to be able to receive messages, which might involve picking the dots and dashes out of a signal loaded with static. Each ship was required to have a radio officer who would command a number of enlisted operators. How should these operators be trained?

When a radio is to be installed on a ship, where do you put it? One thought was that the equipment should be protected as much as possible. This would mean placing it below the main deck behind armor protection. At the same time, the antenna had to be placed as high as possible to obtain the best range. These two factors increased the distance between antenna and receiver, which also increased signal losses. With the radio room located some distance from the bridge or conning tower, communications would require the use of voice tubes and telephones. Others felt that a protected radio room should be located up in the conning tower to improve communications with the captain.

Both in the years leading up to and then during World War I, the technology continued to evolve and improve and the Navy gained much experience in the use of radio. It was the interwar years, however, that showed how much improvement was necessary in the ways that the radio was being used. The problems that had to be solved showed up in the Fleet Problems that were conducted between 1923 and 1940.

The purpose of these large naval exercises was to provide operational experience, experiment with new tactics and determine the best ways to use new technologies. One such technology was radio, but there was also much interest in the use of aircraft and aircraft carriers. The Fleet Problems were held in many locations: the Atlantic Ocean, the Caribbean and the vicinity of the Panama Canal, but mostly in the Pacific Ocean ranging from Alaska to Hawaii and over to Central America. A certain objective would be defined, with one portion of the Fleet as the aggressor and another portion as the defender.

Just to give one example, the objective of Fleet Problem IX held in January 1929 was to attack the Panama Canal. The aircraft carrier *Saratoga* was part of the aggressor (BLACK) forces. In a daring plan, the *Saratoga* and a cruiser were detached from the rest of the BLACK forces and proceeded to the launch point for their attack. The attacking aircraft arrived unopposed over the Canal and succeeded in "destroying" several of the locks.

This successful attack was taken to indicate the future potential of the aircraft carrier. What is sometimes omitted is that the BLUE forces had intercepted a radio message from *Saratoga* that she had arrived at her launch position. When ships were spotted by the *Saratoga*, they were not the ships of the BLACK force arriving to protect her. They were ships of the BLUE forces that had used the intercepted message to determine her location. Although her attack on the Canal had succeeded, the *Saratoga* was "sunk" by the defenders.

Interception of radio signals was an important concern. Even if an intercepted signal could not be decoded or used to provide a precise fix on the enemy's location, it was an indication that he was out there in a certain direction. Fleet Problems indicated other communication difficulties. Messages had to be encrypted to prevent the enemy from knowing their content and then decrypted by the recipient. Delays that occurred in both processes led to suggestions that there were occasions when plain language radio messages should be used for sending important information in the midst of battle.

Ships had to communicate with each other under normal conditions, but sending too many messages would tend to clog the system. A message broadcast from the fleet commander, for example, originally required that every ship reply to indicate that it had received the message. One step taken to reduce the number of messages was the "no receipt" method. It had two disadvantages. There was no way for the sender to know if everyone had received a particular message. There was also no way for any ship to know that it had received all messages. The solution was to assign numbers to the messages so that it would be clear that something had not been received.

The preceding paragraphs have given only an extremely brief look at some of the difficulties that arose following the introduction of radio into the United States Navy. For those with a desire to learn more, I strongly recommend *Information at Sea* by Timothy S. Wolters.

From the early days of radio, it was evident that the electromagnetic waves were being affected by physical objects. By 1904, in Germany, Christian Hülsmeyer had proposed a system that ships could use to detect objects that posed a danger of collision. A signal would be generated by a spark gap transmitter and the received reflected signal would be used to indicate the presence of an object. His problem was the primitive state of the technology, particularly the lack of sensitivity of the receiver. In 1917, Nikola Tesla also suggested the use of radio waves reflected from some object.

I will focus on the activities of the United States Navy and the NRL. An experiment done on communications in 1922 had a transmitter and a receiver located on opposite shores of the Potomac river. During the test, it was observed that a ship passing down the river was interfering with the signals. Research was performed at NRL in pursuit of the principle of detection of objects into the 1930s.

Early radio detection systems had two serious limitations for naval use. The size of the antenna is related to the frequency being transmitted and received. The lower the frequency, the larger the antenna must be. The frequencies being employed in early tests required antennas too large for shipboard use. These early systems used two antennas: one connected to the transmitter and one connected to the receiver. If both had been connected to the same antenna, the powerful transmitter output would have burned out the sensitive receiver input.

The efforts of the NRL in increasing the frequencies of radio communication systems helped to devise ways to make these experimental detection systems also work at higher frequencies. As the frequency of operation increased, the antenna would get smaller. Devices were then developed at the NRL and elsewhere that would isolate the input of the receiver from the powerful transmitted signal but then allow the faint signal reflected from the distant object to be passed to the input. This permitted the use of only one antenna.

These developments led to the construction and comparison of two systems in early 1939. At this point, I will begin to refer to these detection systems as radars, although the term did not come into official use until the following year. The two radars were the XAF constructed by the NRL and CXZ constructed by the Radio Corporation of America (RCA). The XAF radar operated at 200 MHz and was installed on the battleship *New York*. The CXZ operated at 385 MHz and was installed on the battleship *Texas*.

The results of the tests made during Fleet Problem XX showed that the XAF was the clear winner. The CXZ was not capable of detecting targets at the ranges exhibited by the XAF. The electrical components of the CXZ did not stand up under the conditions at sea and its operation was affected by the firing of the big guns of the *Texas*. Most of the faults of the CXZ were attributed to the fact that it had been designed and built in a hurry.

One very important part of the use of the XAF in the Fleet Problem must be mentioned. Four "enemy" destroyers approached the *New York* at night, apparently safe under the cover of darkness. What the commanders of the destroyers did not know was that they were being tracked by radar. The radar information was used to aim the *New York*'s searchlights. When the searchlights were switched on, they were right on target, catching the destroyers by surprise. When this exercise was repeated at a later date, the destroyers were tracked but the information did not reach the searchlight operators. It became clear that even a promising technology such as radar required that the information it provided must be handled in the proper manner.

The Navy made the decision to have RCA build 20 copies of the XAF. The first six such radars were called CXAM and were to be delivered by mid-1940. The remaining radars were a slightly improved version called the CXAM-1 and were to be delivered in 1941. With these radar orders in place, we can now take a look at the writings of science fiction author Edward Elmer "Doc" Smith.

E. E. Smith (1890 – 1965) properly deserved the title of "Doc" as he possessed a Ph.D. in Chemical Engineering with a focus on food engineering. The title of his 1919 dissertation at George Washington University was "The effect of bleaching with oxides of nitrogen upon the baking quality and commercial value of wheat flour."

In 1915, he began work on a novel involving interstellar travel, enlisting Lee Garby, the wife of a friend, to help him with the romantic aspects of the story. The story was abandoned in 1916 by Smith and Garby when only partially completed. He resumed work on it in 1919, completing *The Skylark of Space* in the spring of 1920. Smith had trouble placing it with any publishers, and it was not until 1927 that it was sold to Hugo Gernsback for appearance in *Amazing Stories* in 1928.

The *Skylark of Space* had three successors: *Skylark Three* in *Amazing Stories* in 1930, *Skylark of Valeron* in *Astounding Stories* in 1934 and 1935 and *Skylark DuQuesne* in *If* in 1965. These stories were concerned with the conflict of Dick Seaton and Martin Crane with villain Blackie Duquesne. The stories were characterized by travel over immense distances and releases of great amounts of energy by weapons of ever increasing power. Another feature of these stories was an utter disregard of certain principles of physics such as the limitation on travel faster than the speed of light.

Of interest here is another collection of novels created by Smith called the Lensman Series. There are six novels in the series, but as originally structured there were only four. *Galactic Patrol* appeared in *Astounding Stories* in 1937 and 1938, *Gray Lensman* in *Astounding Science-Fiction* in 1939 and 1940, *Second Stage Lensmen* in *Astounding Science-Fiction* in 1941 and 1942 and *Children of the Lens* in *Astounding Science Fiction* in 1947 and 1948. *Triplanetary*, which originally appeared in *Amazing Stories* in 1934, was not part of the Lensman series. It was modified in 1948 to make it the first in the series. A sixth novel, *First Lensman*, appeared in 1950 to fit between the modified *Triplanetary* and *Galactic Patrol*.

The Lensman series is basically a battle between good, as represented by a peaceful race called the Arisians, and evil, as represented by a race called the Eddorians. The key weapon on the side of good is the Lens, created by the mental science of the Arisians. Only the person to whom a Lens has been issued can use it; death is the result to anyone else trying to use a Lens. Two Lensmen can communicate instantly over any distance (again Smith ignored the speed of light limit). The Lens also allows its wearer to communicate with any other being. Although the stories naturally focus on the activities of human Lensmen such as Kimball Kinnison, there are also non-human Lensmen.

Here we encounter the problem of battle management. The novels of the Lensman series involved space battles between fleets of incredible size. It was discovered during a mission involving a small fleet of *only* 50,000 ships that control was impossible. Even though that particular battle was won, the decision was made to design and construct a means of controlling 1,000,000 ships.

The starting point for the management of the immensely large battle fleet was what Smith described as part of every pilot room – a three-dimensional galactic chart called a "tank." According to the *Gray Lensman*, the final version of the tank was 700 feet in diameter and 80 feet high in the middle with a volume of 17,000,000 cubic feet. The tank appeared on the cover of the November 1939 issue of *Astounding Science-Fiction*, as shown in Figure 12. It was housed in a special ship, the *Z9M9Z*, which was also called the *Directrix*.

In *Gray Lensman*, it was explained that initially there seemed to be no way of handling the large mass of information presented by the tank. The means of solving this problem was not explained to the reader in any

Figure 12. Cover of the November 1939 issue of *Astounding Science-Fiction* featuring "Gray Lensman" by E. E. "Doc" Smith. Cover by Hubert Rogers. Copyright © 2018 by Penny Publications LLC/Dell Magazines.

comprehensible manner, but evidence was given that everything was soon working as desired:

> Red lights are fleets already in motion . . . Greens are fleets still at their bases. Ambers are the planets the greens took off from – connected, you see, by Ryerson string-lights. The white star is us, the *Directrix*. That violet cross way over there is Jalte's planet, our first objective. The pink comets are our free planets, their tails showing their intrinsic velocities. Being so slow, they had to start long ago. The purple circle is the negasphere. It's on its way, too.

An important feature of the system was a much smaller version of the tank called a reducer. It would enable the Admiral in charge to view the overall scope of the battle without being able to distinguish the smaller features at all. Any order that he issued would be acted on by the army of technicians manning the full-sized tank.

A brief conversation between Kinnison and the Admiral indicated the advantage that was conveyed by the battle management system. The Admiral began by mentioning the earlier battle that indicated the need for the new system:

> If, as I believe much more likely, they have no better Grand Fleet Operations than we had in Helmuth's star-cluster – if they haven't the equivalent of you and Worsel and this supertank here – then what?

To which Kinnison replied:

> In that case it'd be just too bad. Just like pushing baby chicks into a pond.

For those of you not familiar with the stories, Worsel was one of the non-human Lensmen: a dragon, thirty feet long, and with wings, talons and scales. The tank and the Directrix were introduced in *Gray Lensman* but were also used in *Second Stage Lensman* and *Children of the Lens*. With the tank now operating properly on board the *Directrix*, let us now return to the radars that were ordered by the Navy.

You will recall that the first batch of radars were designated CXAM and were to be delivered in 1940. They were installed on the aircraft carrier *Yorktown*, the battleship *California*, and the cruisers *Chicago*, *Chester*, *Pensacola* and *Northampton*. As was said earlier with regard to the first installations of radios on ships, when one installs a new piece of equipment on a ship there are many problems to consider.

Each of the ships that received the CXAM radars tried to fit it into the existing systems. On the battleship *California*, the Captain authorized his Communications Officer, Lieutenant Commander Henry Bernstein, to create a radar plotting room. This facility included the display unit of the CXAM radar, two voice radios, a horizontal plotting table, a radio direction finder and telephones for communication around the ship.

The Captain of the carrier *Yorktown* sent a report to the Commander in Chief, Pacific Fleet in which he pointed out the problems that been encountered in using radar. The men operating the radar sent range and bearing information obtained from the radar by phone to Flag Plot, the bridge and other units for each to work with as needed. There was no central plotting facility to present an overall picture. In the absence of such a facility, he observed that there was no way for a person receiving such information to form a useful mental picture of the battle. This required the formation of radar plotting teams and creation of adequate physical facilities for assimilating and segregating vital information.

The men on these first six ships were all working with radar and finding out what worked and what didn't. Reports and recommendations were passed up the chain of command. This type of activity increased after the 14 CXAM-1 radars began arriving in 1941.

It was recognized that the introduction of radar would present problems in training and maintenance that would exceed those that had been required by radio. It was not reasonable to expect men to learn on the job how to detect and identify enemy forces and take the appropriate action. Schools had to be developed for both the enlisted men and officers. Fortunately, these schools had been started before the United States entered the war and were quickly expanded to supply the wartime demand.

A limitation of the early radars was the way that the information was displayed. The Type A or A-scope display used a horizontal trace across the display. The left end of the trace represented the location of the radar. When a radar pulse was emitted, the trace would begin to sweep across the screen to the right. This occurred many times in one second as determined by the pulse repetition rate of the radar. If the radar signal was reflected by some object, the received echo would cause a spike, a vertical deflection of the trace, above the horizontal line. The position of the spike indicated the range of the object causing the reflection. If, for example, the full width of the trace corresponded to 150 miles, a spike halfway across was from an object at a range of 75 miles.

A serious limitation of the A-scope display was that it only showed what was in the direction that the antenna was pointing. A radar operator tracking one target would have no indication of another target coming from a different direction. He would also have to look at a second indicator to learn which way the antenna was pointed. This problem was solved by a type of display developed independently by the British and the U.S. Navy (at NRL). It was called the Plan Position Indicator (PPI). This system employs a continually rotating antenna to obtain a full 360-degree view. The radar display is synchronized with the rotation of the antenna. Each trace starts from the center of the display and continues to the outer edge. Think of a wagon wheel with a very large number of thin spokes. If a target is detected, the echo causes a brightening of the trace. The operator then has a view of objects that surround the radar in the center of the display. If the term radar is mentioned, this is the type of display with which most people are probably familiar.

How do you convey complex battle information as gathered by radar to the captain and others on the ship? Attempting to explain such complex information by telephone was not a suitable approach. After the introduction of the PPI, one suggested approach was to make tracings of the displays and take them to the bridge. Again, not a very practical solution. It was then realized that if you could present the information on one display in the radar plotting room, the same information could be electronically repeated on similar displays in other locations around the ship. These displays, logically called repeaters, were the solution.

A radar display shows a collection of moving blobs of light that represent ships and planes. In the confusion of battle, how do you tell friendly forces from those of the enemy, particularly aircraft? The basic solution involved equipping each friendly plane with a radio transmitter that would be triggered by the radar beam. The ship would receive the radar echo and also a signal from the triggered transmitter. The electronics would then associate the radio signal with the echo and indicate that a particular object on the screen was friendly. The name assigned to such systems was Identification Friend or Foe (IFF). IFF systems were developed by both the British and the United States.

Although he was mentioned in Chapter 7, I will now introduce Caleb Barrett Laning (1906 – 1991). He graduated from the Naval Academy in 1929, which made him a classmate (and lifelong friend) of science fiction author Robert Heinlein. The following, taken from his Naval Biography, gives his naval career from graduation until the fall of 1942:

Following graduation from the Naval Academy in 1929, he joined the USS *Oklahoma* to serve until November 1932, interspersed with instruction, January - May 1931, in fire control (specialized in Antiaircraft Directors) at the Ford Instrument Company, Long Island, New York. Completing submarine training at the Submarine Base, New London, Connecticut, he reported in June 1933 on board the USS *S-13* and in September 1935 transferred to the USS *R-2*.

He attended a course in general line at the Postgraduate School, Annapolis, Maryland, from June 1936 until May 1938, after which he had duty as Radio Officer on the staff of Commander Cruiser Division Eight, USS *Philadelphia*, flagship. In that capacity, he took part in some of the earliest micro-wave radio experiments in the Fleet. In September 1940 he was assigned to the USS *Sicard* as Executive Officer and received a commendatory letter for his contributions toward the *Sicard*'s winning the Battle Efficiency Pennant in gunnery, engineering and mine laying in 1940. In June 1941 he joined the USS *Conyngham* to serve as Executive Officer and Navigator until October 1942.

A minor correction to Laning's Naval Biography is required. Based on his service record, his postgraduate work was in Applied Communications, not General Line. The General Line course prepared line officers to serve as a shipboard department head or as a commanding officer of small craft. At the time of Laning's postgraduate work, a full year of General Line courses would have been followed by a full year of technical courses. Starting in 1938, more technical courses were given the first year, with a corresponding reduction in General Line courses.

The *Conyngham* was present at Pearl Harbor at the time of the Japanese attack. During the Battle of Midway, she was part of Task Force 16 formed around the carriers *Enterprise* and *Hornet*. When the Task Force separated into two task groups on the morning of June 4, the *Conyngham* was part of the *Hornet* task group.

Returning to Laning's Naval Biography, we are told that his next assignment was as Communications Officer on the staff of Commander Destroyers, U.S. Pacific Fleet, and later also on the staff of Commander Cruisers, U.S. Pacific Fleet. As his postgraduate education had been in Applied Communications you might consider this a reasonable assignment. But just what were his duties?

Laning's Commanding Officer during this time was Rear Admiral Mahlon Tisdale. While a Captain, Tisdale served as CO of the cruiser *Chester* from November 1940 to April 1941. You may recall that *Chester* was one of the ships that received a CXAM radar in 1940. Tisdale was then the Commandant of Midshipmen at the Naval Academy until October

1942. Promoted to Rear Admiral, he became Commander of Cruiser Division 4. Under his command, ships of Cruiser Division 4 were involved in many of the battles connected with the efforts to drive the Japanese from the island of Guadalcanal: The Battle of the Santa Cruz Islands, The Naval Battle of Guadalcanal and The Battle of Tassafaronga. In January 1943, Tisdale was made Commander Destroyers, U.S. Pacific Fleet. A few months later, he was also made Commander Cruisers, U.S. Pacific Fleet. While it appears from his Naval Biography that Laning had jobs on two staffs, both jobs were under Tisdale.

Based on experience gained in the early use of radar, the experiments tried on various ships and combat experience early in the war, the simple Radar Plot had evolved into what is now called the Combat Information Center (CIC). The creation of such a facility on every warship was the purpose of a Tactical Bulletin issued on Thanksgiving Day 1942. The original suggestion for its name, as put forward by Admiral Nimitz, was the Combat *Operations* Center (COC). Objections were raised that operations were directed from locations such as the bridge of the ship. As a result, the name was changed to CIC.

By late 1942, there was a consensus as to what equipment would be needed in a CIC. This would include radars for detecting both ships and aircraft, sonar for detecting submarines and plotting boards for both surface and air contacts. The surface plot would be based on the dead reckoning tracer (DRT) that indicated own-ship's position. Communication facilities would consist of voice tubes, a number of dedicated telephone circuits, and radio equipment.

It was possible to arrive at an ideal arrangement that allowed for the best operating conditions and most efficient flow of information. On larger ships, such as battleships and cruisers, there might not be too much difficulty in finding the room for such an installation. On smaller ships, however, the available suitable space was limited. Laning and other members of Tisdale's staff had to find the best internal arrangement of a Combat Information Center for a destroyer.

This task was made more complicated by the existence of a number of destroyer classes in service. Variations existed between classes in the purpose, size and location of ship's compartments. An arrangement that would be ideal for ships of one class might be impossible to realize with another class. A proposal for the location of a CIC on a ship already in service required the shuffling of existing facilities and quarters. After developing such a proposal, it had to be sent to Bureau of Ships and other command authorities for approval. In a number of cases, all of their work was undone by official disapproval of some feature of their proposed layout.

The work done by Laning was not restricted to the problem of the best arrangement of a Combat Information Center. A look at various memos to and from Laning at this time shows his involvement with the problem of training. Obviously, junior officers and enlisted personnel had to be trained to run the CIC. But what would happen if the Captain and Executive Officer of their ship had no experience or training with regard to CIC? It was also necessary to provide special training to make these senior officers aware of the benefits possible from the CIC and the best way to make use of the information that they were given.

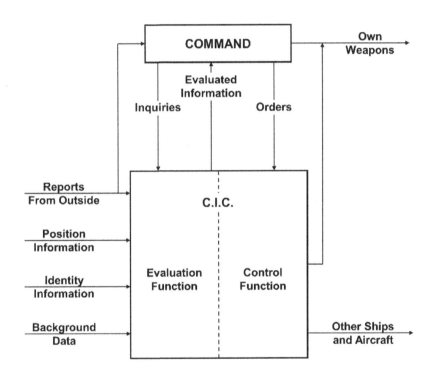

Figure 13. Functional representation of the Combat Information Center. Diagram taken from the *CIC Handbook for Destroyers*.

An important step in making everyone aware of the objectives and procedures was the creation of the "CIC Handbook for Destroyers" by J. C. Wylie, another member of Tisdale's staff. This document was issued in

June 1943. It provided an excellent functional representation of a Combat Information Center, which was used as the basis for Figure 13.

A good way to summarize all of Caleb Laning's valuable contributions during this assignment is to quote from the citation for the Legion of Merit that he received:

His development and completion of vital Combat Information Center Equipment in destroyers materially contributed to an effective destroyer offensive in the Pacific Theatre. By expeditious development of CIC doctrine and organization he materially shortened the period necessary for its full utilization in combat. In addition he evolved a considerable portion of the special techniques and training facilities thus further contributing to its marked success. By an intensive training program to qualify destroyer officers for intercept, and by pressing for the incorporation of facilities in destroyer CIC for fighter direction he contributed materially to a markedly advantageous employment of destroyers.

Following his work on the Combat Information Center, Laning returned to sea duty as Captain of the destroyer *Hutchins*. In January 1944, he wrote the following to his friend Robert Heinlein:

For info, I have been the top man in "CIC" development for past year. You will be fascinated with the story, when it can be told. Basic ideas were frequently very similar to some of Amazing S.F. "brain-machine" ideas. And it works and sinks & shoots down Japs. Save yourself for some super-stories.

As Captain of the *Hutchins*, Laning was present at the Battle of Surigao Strait in October 1944. In 1945, his next posting was to Washington, D.C., in the Radar Section, Electronics Division, Office of the Chief of Naval Operations. Following the war, he had a variety of postings at sea and ashore before retiring as a Rear Admiral in 1959.

I hope that I have been able to show that Caleb Laning was a very important contributor to the success of the Combat Information Center. It should also be clear from the very short history of the use of radar by the Navy I have presented that he was not the originator of the idea. If you wish to find originators, you should perhaps look at the officers and men involved in the earliest work with the CXAM and CXAM-1 radars. They were the ones who came up with the ideas and suggestions that eventually led to the CIC.

During the time that this early experience was being gained in the use of radar, Laning was serving on the *Sicard* and then the *Conyngham*. Neither of those ships had any connection with the CXAM or CXAM-1 radars. It is only in his next assignment that his connection with radar and CIC occurred. It is important to note that Laning only said to Heinlein that he had been involved in CIC *development*.

One final comment about the origin of the Combat Information Center worth presenting is taken from the Preface of the *CIC Handbook*:

> The development of the Combat Information Center as an integral unit of the ship's organization is possibly one of the most drastic and rapid changes in our shipboard experience. Apparently, the need for such an agency, a tactical plot or a ship's operations officer, existed before the war without our general realization of the fact. When radar was developed, it simply furnished us with more information than we were able to handle in any way other than with this tactical plotting and evaluating agency. This is the origin of the C.I.C. It is not the child of theory, it is a proven result of combat experience.

How does the Combat Information Center compare with what was presented by the writings of Doc Smith? There are four points of comparison.

The problem in both cases was one of management of a complex battle situation. The fictional solution was a massive system that took in and analyzed the information so that the entire battle could be directed from the *Directrix*. The Navy's solution was also to bring in the information but on the smallest scale possible, with a center of analysis and direction on each ship.

How do you present the data to those who must make the decisions? In the Lensman stories, it was by using the massive tank. The Navy made use of radar displays, most likely employing the PPI, plus plotting boards and tables.

How was the information displayed in other locations? The fictional Admiral Haynes made use of the reducer, which presented the information from the main tank in a much smaller scale. A captain on the bridge of a ship would have made use of the repeater, which presented the same image as the display in CIC.

Finally, how do you distinguish between friends and enemies? By the quote taken from *Gray Lensman*, this was accomplished by some unexplained means, but objects were displayed in the tank in different colors according to their identity. The Navy made use of IFF circuitry that would cause objects on the radar display to be appropriately labeled.

Why should such a comparison even be necessary? It is necessary because it has been claimed that the CIC was based on the writings of Doc Smith. This claim is based on a letter dated June 11, 1947 from John W. Campbell Jr., the editor of *Astounding Science Fiction* to Doc Smith.

Campbell began the letter by saying it was private and personal but that it was something Smith deserved to hear. He told Smith that he had made a major contribution in helping to win the war. To back up this assertion, he gave a reasonably accurate description of the purpose and operation of a Combat Information Center. This was followed by these four paragraphs:

> CIC was introduced into the Navy scheme by a navy officer who was not then, nor is not now, able to explain to the Navy precisely where he got the idea. Unofficially, and in confidence, he has told me.

> The entire set-up was taken specifically, directly, and consciously from the "Directrix". In your story, you reached the situation the Navy was in---more communications channels than integration techniques to handle it. You proposed such an integrating technique, and proved how advantageous it could be.

> You, sir, were 100% right. As the Japanese Navy---not the hypothetical Boskonian fleet---learned at an appalling cost. Sitting in Michigan, some years before Pearl Harbor, you played a large share in the greatest and most decisive naval action of the recent war!

> Unfortunately, in order that a Naval officer with imagination enough to apply the science-fiction ideas he studies may continue to have the maximum possible influence on the Navy, the source of his ideas---a source the Brass Hats wouldn't take to so well--- must remain undisclosed. He's Capt. Cal Lanning. At present, he is in charge of all Naval electronic research, with special emphasis on advanced spy ray equipment, detector screens, and detector screen analysis techniques.

This concentration on CIC was then followed by a general discussion of ways in which an enemy may be deceived. Campbell's closing sentence said that Smith should not spread the word about the connection between the Directrix and CIC so that Laning could continue to base future developments on science fiction.

A portion of Smith's letter was used after his death by his daughter, Verna Smith Trestrail, in a speech given at a science fiction convention in 1979. Then a portion of her speech was used in the 2008 book *Different Engines*, which stated that Smith had influenced military strategy. In putting forward this claim, a slightly modified version of the second paragraph above was presented. Quite a major error was made by the authors of this book in attributing the letter to Admiral Nimitz rather than Campbell. It was also said that Campbell spread the story around, which conflicts with his actual closing statement to Smith. Here I will only be concerned with what Campbell said and possibly why he said it.

Campbell began by claiming that the CIC was introduced to the Navy by a single officer with whom he had been in contact. As I have briefly shown here, but which can also be seen in much greater detail from available references and documents, the introduction of CIC was the work of many, not one. Regarding his contact with the officer, I will come back to that.

Campbell then claimed that the "set-up" was consciously taken from the *Directrix*. Again, evidence clearly exists that CIC grew out of the experiences and suggestions that followed the introduction of radar into the United States Navy. There is no real evidence anywhere that shows that it came from works of science fiction written by Smith or anyone else.

Consider that the Navy was facing the same problem proposed by Smith in his stories – How do you manage a complex battle? Allowing that the circumstances of the combat were somewhat different, it is not surprising to me that two independent solutions were developed with the points of similarity that I listed above. That two such similar solutions exist does not automatically mean that one solution was derived from the other.

I think that you will agree that we may simply ignore Campbell's third paragraph. The fourth paragraph contains a number of errors. The most obvious is that he misspelled Laning's name. Since we know that Laning was not responsible for introducing a concept derived from science fiction, Campbell's plea to keep the source of such concepts secret from Laning's superiors has no meaning. It is further known that although Laning was in the Electronics Division of the office of the CNO, his specialty was radar. He was clearly not in charge of ALL electronics research. I will leave it to you to decide what Campbell meant by "advanced spy ray equipment, detector screens, and detector screen analysis techniques."

I interpret the first paragraph to indicate that Campbell had a face-to-face meeting with Laning. Such a meeting, if it existed, most likely would have been arranged by Robert Heinlein. Unfortunately, no record of the date and place of such a meeting has yet been discovered. If it was only written communication, it has not been located either. Of course, we have no way of knowing exactly what Laning told Campbell. I am positive, however, that Laning did not make any of the claims presented by Campbell that we now know to be incorrect.

Campbell was always interested in showing how science fiction had an influence on the real world. He would have been very pleased to show that science fiction had affected the course of the war. From Laning's comment to Heinlein in January 1944 and other sources, it is known that he read science fiction. I consider it possible that he used science fiction and even the works of Doc Smith to explain the operation of CIC to Campbell. You will note that in the 1944 comment to Heinlein, Laning said that CIC was "similar" to ideas from science fiction. He did not say that it was based on science fiction.

So why did Campbell write what he did to Smith? One possibility is simply faulty memory on the part of Campbell. If he and Laning did have a meeting instead of just written communication, such faulty recall becomes more likely. There is also Campbell's desire to bolster the reputation of science fiction. In any case, it appears that any similarities between CIC and the works of Doc Smith, either stated by Laning or inferred from what he said, were converted in Campbell's mind to direct influences. This is what formed the basis of what he wrote to Smith. Campbell's statements have only served to obscure the real contributions made by many people, *including Caleb Laning*, in either the creation or development of the Combat Information Center.

9

WRITE OR INVENT?

The previous chapters have each looked at the question of inspiration of an inventor by a story created by a science fiction author. In each of the cases that was investigated, the author was a different person than the inventor. This naturally brings up the question, can we find science fiction authors who were or are also inventors?

Of course we can.

The science fiction author that most people will identify with inventions is Hugo Gernsback (1884 – 1967). He was born in Luxembourg, the youngest of three sons of a successful wine merchant. He developed an early interest in electricity and while quite young had a business installing simple electrical devices and systems in homes and buildings in the region around his home.

As a boy, Gernsback was educated by private tutors. He then attended an industrial school, a boarding school in Brussels and then the Rheinisches Technikum in Bingen am Rhein, Germany. There he studied mathematics and electrical engineering. He developed a very powerful battery and decided that the United States was the best place to seek his fortune. In 1903, the year that he completed his studies, his father died. He had no interest in running the family wine business, which was taken over by his brother and a cousin (his other brother having died in 1891).

After he arrived in New York, he found that while his battery was powerful, it would cost too much to manufacture. He became involved with a number of businesses concerned with batteries and other electrical components. He then founded The Electric Importing Company to import equipment from Europe. In 1908, he brought out a radio magazine called

Modern Electrics "to teach the young generation science, radio and what was ahead for them."

Let us step back from the magazine for a moment and consider Gernsback's life as an inventor. In his obituary, it was claimed that he had 80 patents. This number continues to be mindlessly repeated on the Internet. I was fortunate to encounter an article in a magazine published by The Antique Wireless Association that listed patents that were issued to early radio pioneers including Gernsback. The number of United States patents held by Gernsback was 37, not 80. This number includes two design patents for a radio cabinet. If the larger number is not simply a value that someone made up, it would have to include patents issued in other countries that most likely duplicated some of the United States patents.

What were some of his patents? As might be expected, some of them were for electrical devices: "Battery Cell" (842,950), "Relay" (978,999), "Potentiometer" (988,456) and "Rotary Variable Condenser" (1,033,095). Some of his other inventions covered quite a range: "Combined Electric Hair Brush and Comb" (1,016,138), "Submersible Amusement Device" (1,384,750), "Apparatus for Landing Flying Machines" (1,392,140) and "Hydraulic Fishery" (2,718,083).

Gernsback published *Modern Electrics* until he sold it in March 1913. By April 1913, he had started a new magazine, *The Electrical Experimenter*. The magazine was renamed *Science and Invention* in 1920 and lasted until 1931, although Gernsback was associated with it only until 1929. All of these magazines contained some works of science fiction. They might have been reprints of works by Poe, Verne or Wells, or they may have been original short works by Gernsback and others.

The first pulp science fiction magazine was *Amazing Stories,* which Gernsback brought out with a cover date of April 1926. This was followed by *Amazing Stories Annual* and *Amazing Stories Quarterly*. After he lost control of his magazines due to bankruptcy proceedings, he formed yet another company and began publishing new science fiction magazines. Over the years, he also published magazines such as *Radio News, Radio-Craft, Sexology* and *Technocracy Review*.

Gernsback was perhaps better known as a publisher than an author. As I said above, some stories in his early magazines were written by him, either under his own name or a pseudonym. His only work of fiction that anyone reads today is the novel *Ralph 124C 41+*, which appeared in *Modern Electrics* from April 1911 to March 1912. It is set in the year 2660 and can best be described as a collection of futuristic inventions that just happens to have a story line running through it.

Did anything he invented appear in any of his stories? I have not gone back through all the fiction that he has written, so I cannot provide an absolute answer. As far as I am able to determine, however, the answer is No. It was claimed in one source that the "hypnobioscope," which appears in *Ralph*, was one of Gernsback's patented inventions. This machine would transmit information directly into the brain while a person slept. No such machine exists. Gernsback later wrote of the related concept of "sleep learning" that claims to convey information by playing a recording to a sleeping person.

One of his inventions was mentioned in the June 1920 issue of *Electrical Experimenter*. The cover shows a Ferris Wheel with the people in enclosed cars travelling down an inclined track into the water. The corresponding article "A Sea-Going Ferris Wheel" was written by Gernsback. It is worth noting that this article appeared a few months before he filed the patent application for the "Submersible Amusement Device."

The next author to consider is Robert Forward (1932 – 2002). He received his Ph.D. in Gravitational Physics from the University of Maryland in 1965. The title of his dissertation was "Detectors for Dynamic Gravitational Fields." From 1956 to 1987, Forward was at the Hughes Aircraft Company Research Laboratories in Malibu, California. In 1987, he left Hughes to form his own company Forward Unlimited for consulting and writing. In 1987, he formed Tethers Unlimited with Dr. Robert Hoyt.

Forward had 28 patents; 18 of these are from his time at Hughes. The Hughes patents cover a range of technical areas, although several seem to be related to gravity, possibly inspired by his graduate research. The last nine are related to tethers, which are long cables that may be used in conjunction with satellites and other types of spacecraft.

The one patent that does not fall in either of the two groups is "Statite: Spacecraft that Utilizes Light Pressure and Method of Use" (5,183,225). There is a minor error in the title of the patent, which says "Sight Pressure." The two factors that determine the orbit of a satellite are its velocity and gravity. The statite makes use of a solar sail oriented such that the light pressure from the Sun is equal and opposite to the gravitational pull of the Earth. This would enable it to be placed in space relative to the Earth without having to be moving in orbit.

All of Forward's fiction may be described as hard science fiction in which the emphasis is on the scientific and technical aspects of the story. Such works include "Dragon's Egg" that looks at life on a neutron star, "Rocheworld" (and its sequels) that begins with a journey to Barnard's

Star and the exploration of two closely coupled planets and "Saturn Rukh" that involves contact with massive creatures living in the atmosphere of Saturn. Some of his early short fiction and newer works were included in *Indistinguishable from Magic*, which explores a number of possible future technologies.

Wil McCarthy (1966 –) has 30 patents. A common theme running through his inventions is that of Programmable Matter, where the properties of the matter can be modified according to some input. Such properties could include density, conductivity or reflectivity.

Some of McCarthy's patents are concerned with quantum dots. What is a quantum dot? We can begin with an element such as silicon. By adding the appropriate impurities known as dopants, we may create either N-type material with an excess of free electrons or P-type with an excess of holes (electron absences that behave as positive particles). By combining N-type and P-type material we can create diodes and transistors.

If we create a PNP structure in which the N layer is very thin, a quantum well is created. This will restrict the movement of electrons to the plane of the N layer. If we then make the upper P layer and the N layer a very narrow strip, we have created a quantum wire. The electrons can now propagate only along the long axis of the wire. But we can go one step further. We can shorten the two layers of the wire until we have confined the electrons in all three dimensions. This is a quantum dot. Incidentally, there are other ways of forming quantum dots.

The electrons confined in the quantum dot will repel each other. They will assume an arrangement depending on the number of electrons, their energies and the size of the dot. The situation is similar to that of electrons surrounding the nucleus of an atom, although no nucleus is present in this case. Quantum dots have potential applications in areas such as solar cells, light emitting diodes and displays. A recent issue of *IEEE Spectrum* featured an article on the use of quantum dots to create very bright color TV displays.

The science fiction of Wil McCarthy employs the themes of nanotechnology and programmable matter. His novels *The Collapsium, Wellstone, Lost in Transmission* and *To Crush the Moon* take programmable matter to extremes. Wellstone is a material that incorporates quantum dots to obtain the desired properties. In *The Collapsium*, a type of wellstone is used to contain billions of tons of neutronium that would otherwise explode.

Another science fiction author to look at is John W. Campbell, Jr. Although he was known as a science fiction author in the 1930s, he is perhaps better known as an editor. He was the editor of *Astounding Science Fiction* (later *Analog*) from 1937 until his death. He was also the editor of the fantasy magazine *Unknown* (later *Unknown Worlds*).

Campbell's only patent was "Electron Discharge Apparatus" (2,954,466). It is a simple circuit of two vacuum tubes for the purpose of generating different waveforms. Depending on the voltages applied to the two inputs of the circuit, it is possible to generate a square wave, a sawtooth or a stepped waveform.

The only mystery concerning this patent is why he went through the trouble to get it. Most of my own work in electronics has involved transistors and integrated circuits, although I did work with vacuum tubes a little bit when I was young. One is always coming up with some new circuit for a special purpose or application. I can speak from experience in that regard. There are books available with page after page of circuits that people have designed. How many of those designers felt that their circuit, however clever, was worthy of a patent? I can only suggest that Campbell simply wanted to be able to say that he had a patent.

There is one more science fiction author and inventor that I now wish to discuss in some detail. The author is William Fitzgerald Jenkins (1896 – 1975), who is perhaps better known by his pen name of Murray Leinster. In a case such as this, which name should be used? Although I will be discussing him both as an author and inventor, the emphasis will be a bit more on the inventor, so I will stick with Jenkins.

Will Jenkins was born in Norfolk, Virginia. He had a half-sister Lula and an older brother George Jr. He would have had three older brothers, but each had died shortly after birth. The family had a good life until Will's father, George Sr., lost his job in 1910. The family moved to New York City, where his father worked as an accountant.

Will, his brother and his mother returned briefly to Norfolk. It is not clear, but it appears that Will's father remained in New York City. By 1912, George Jr. was working for the Prudential Insurance Company in Newark, New Jersey. Because of the many moves, Will was unable to attend school regularly. His formal education ended at the eighth grade. He went to work at Prudential Insurance Company as an office boy.

His career as a writer began when he submitted epigrams to *The Smart Set*, a literary magazine. He also began to submit other material including poems and stories to *The Smart Set* and also to other magazines such as *The Parisienne*, *Saucy Stories* and *Snappy Stories*. Following a disagreement with his boss at Prudential, he quit his job.

Both Will and his brother George had registered for the draft in World War I. George was sent overseas, but Will remained stateside and was sent to the Office of Public Information in a training unit. During this time his work continued to appear in his usual magazines. He also began selling stories to *Argosy* and *All-Story Weekly*.

The science fiction career of Will Jenkins began with the story "The Runaway Skyscraper" that appeared in the February 22, 1919 issue of *Argosy*. This is not to imply that from that point on he just wrote science fiction. Far from it. If you look at his bibliography, you will also find mysteries, adventures and westerns. These appeared as by Will Jenkins, Will F. Jenkins, William Fitzgerald and Murray Leinster. He even wrote romances under the name of Louisa Carter Lee. It is said that his published works amount to 1500 short stories and almost 100 books.

Although his formal education ended at the eighth grade, Jenkins was self-educated and very well read. His house on the north bank of the York river in Virginia was filled with books on a wide range of subjects. If his deficiencies in the area of formal education did not prevent him from becoming a successful author, it also appears not to have hurt his career as an inventor.

One period for which there exists a lot of information about the inventive nature of Will Jenkins was World War II. The way to begin is to look at his fellow science fiction author Robert Heinlein. In January 1942, Heinlein had been contacted by his friend and former shipmate Albert "Buddy" Scoles, who was Assistant Chief Engineer for Materials at the Naval Aircraft Factory (NAF) in Philadelphia. In his letter, Scoles asked if Heinlein was interested in working at the NAF. He also suggested that science fiction authors and readers might be able to provide solutions to wartime technical problems. In April 1942, Heinlein wrote to Scoles that he had received a list of such ideas from Will Jenkins and that he had enclosed the list with the letter. He said:

> If I understand your original notion in wanting me to dig up science-fiction writers with ideas, this is the sort of memo you have been wanting to get—with the expectation that ninetynine ideas would be lousy but the hundredth might prove to be a doozy.

Unfortunately, there is no way to know what was on that list.

Later in 1942, Jenkins did provide some specific ideas regarding the pressure suits needed for high-altitude work. This was the problem that Scoles had mentioned in his letter to Heinlein. One could think of a pressure suit as a type of balloon. The higher air pressure within the suit would cause it to assume its fully inflated shape with arms, legs and hands fully extended. Unless the suit was properly designed, the person wearing it would have to constantly work against this inflated shape to be able to do anything useful.

One of the suggestions made by Jenkins was based on the toy in the shape of a woven bamboo tube. You insert your fingers into the ends of the tube. If you pull, the tube pattern tightens and you cannot release your fingers. To release them, you must press inward, which causes the tube to expand. He suggested that some woven material could be used in the suit that would resist changes in length or diameter. His second suggestion was not directly related to the design of the suit. He suggested that the air supply for a pressure suit could be extended by using some of the air in the tank to help run a compressor to put air back into the tank.

In July 1942, Jenkins went to work for the Office of War Information. This was a government agency that operated both Domestic and Overseas Branches. The Domestic Branch produced radio shows dealing with the war, made newsreels and established the Voice of America. The Overseas Branch attempted to undermine the morale of the Axis forces and population and to provide assistance to those who were supporting the Allied cause.

Jenkins's work appears to have been in connection with the Overseas Branch. In July 1943, he requested permission to travel to Washington. The purpose of the trip was to demonstrate some "OWI gadgets" that he had developed to the Army and Navy. They were for use by the underground in Europe. The first gadget involved sheets of paper with prepared text, from which many copies could be made without any equipment. All that was required was a supply of ink or pigment. The second gadget was a variation of the first, with blank sheets on which messages could be created using a pencil and then duplicated. The third was a means of creating metal printing plates from text or images in just five minutes.

In a letter to Robert Heinlein in July 1945, Jenkins presented an idea for improving the effectiveness of bombing. His claim was that if two explosive devices were located such that each was in the other's blast area and detonated at the same time, the results would be more destructive than if they were detonated separately. Jenkins said this would work even if the second device was set off by the explosion of the first. He proposed dropping a series of bombs that would not explode on impact. After they were all in position, the first would be detonated to trigger the rest. My view of this idea is that it might not be possible to drop a group of bombs close enough to each other to guarantee that the blast of each would trigger the next.

139

Jenkins said that he came up with an idea for reducing the wake behind a submarine periscope. Using a stick moving through the water in a bathtub to simulate a periscope, he found that a collection of ribbons tied to the stick would smooth out the water and eliminate the wake. He managed to pass the idea on to the Navy. The story is that one admiral commented, "I understand that the inventor speaks of experimenting with the device in a bathtub, what did he use for a periscope?"

In his Guest of Honor speech at the 1963 Worldcon, Jenkins mentioned an idea he proposed for fighting the kamikazes. This idea was passed on to Robert Heinlein in Philadelphia. It involved a shell that contained one charge to create a dense smoke cloud and a second charge to ignite magnesium particles. The charge to create the smoke cloud would fire first. The second charge would fire after the shell had passed through the smoke cloud, lighting up the sky. This would supposedly make it easier to spot the enemy planes. According to Jenkins, the test of the idea was never performed because the war ended. I feel that there are some problems with the story as he told it, primarily with regard to the role of Heinlein in testing the idea.

He may have provided other ideas regarding the kamikazes. In 1946, Robert Heinlein wrote to his friend, naval officer Cal Laning. During the last months of the war, Heinlein and other science fiction authors had been sending ideas to Laning regarding ways of combating the kamikazes. In the letter, Heinlein asked:

> Did you send Will Jenkins that acknowledgement of his anti-kamikaze efforts or not? You told me that you intended to but I have never known. All that is needed is a simple note, on official stationary, over your signature, thanking him for his patriotic efforts in supplying, when requested, ideas intended to repel kamikaze attacks.

In a 1963 letter, Jenkins mentioned two other wartime ideas. The first involved the use of buoys with microphones and transmitters to help track submarines. He was told by the Navy that they were not interested, but later found that such a system had been developed independently and placed in use. The second idea was a fire alarm system for aircraft that was supposedly patented by someone else. No other details are known.

This brief look at his wartime activities clearly demonstrates that Jenkins had an extremely inventive mind. There are stories and anecdotes by other people that mention ideas that he had supposedly developed. But there is no hard evidence to support these stories. A bit of research has shown that he only had two patents. This was verified by one of his daughters. Over the years, he may have brought many other ideas to a successful result. In such cases, he could have simply sold or licensed the idea to someone without bothering to obtain a patent

But what about those two patents? They are "Apparatus for Production of Light Effects in Composite Photography" (2,727,427) and "Apparatus for the Production of Composite Photographic Effects" (2,727,429). We know the story about these patents because of an article that Jenkins wrote. This was "Applied Science Fiction" that appeared in the November 1967 issue of *Analog*.

According to the article, the idea was born when he was watching the production of one of his stories for a television series. In a discussion with the producer, he became aware of the limitations of physical scenery. He knew of the use of rear projection to create a background but was also aware of some of its limitations. The image projected from behind a translucent screen had to be very bright to permit it to be photographed. Any stray light had to be avoided on the front of the screen.

He wondered if the scenery could somehow be projected from the front. The first answer would seem to be no, as the scenery would project onto the actors as well. But Jenkins continued to pursue the idea. He commented that:

> But I was a science-fiction writer. (I still am.) A mere impossibility did not bother me. I considered the situation as if I were planning a story in terms of a device. For a story, a device need only to seem plausible. Whether or not it works doesn't matter. And this is how the whole thing started.

The answer came from his recognition that there are different types of reflection. There is specular (or what he called metallic) reflection such as from a mirror. There is diffuse reflection, which is the means by which light reaches us from most objects around us. Then there is retroreflection (or reflex reflection) in which light is returned in the direction from which it originated.

A retroreflector can be made by mounting three mirrors at right angles to each other. The corner reflector will return light striking it from any angle back where it came from. Another type of retroreflector is based on glass spheres with an appropriate refractive index. The sphere surface will then behave as a concave spherical mirror. A retroreflective surface is made when small retroreflective glass beads or microprisms are placed on fabric or a sheet of plastic.

After some experimentation with a small sheet of retroreflective material, Jenkins arrived at the design shown in Figure 14. The view of the system is from above.

The desired background image is sent out by the projector P. It strikes the half-silvered mirror M. Some of the light passes through the mirror and is lost, but the rest is reflected towards the main screen S1, which is made of retroreflective material. The reflected light follows the same path back to the mirror. Some of the light passes through the mirror to the camera C. There will be some losses due to partial reflection and passage through the mirror, but the background image that the camera sees will be very bright.

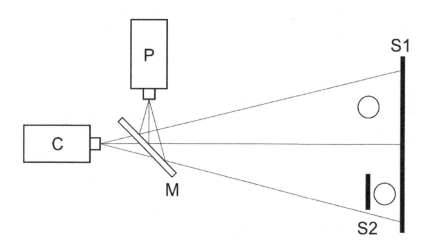

Figure 14. Front Projection system as developed by Will Jenkins. Based on diagrams in patent 2,727,427.

But what about the actors in the scene, as represented by the upper circle in Figure 14? The light will be diffusely reflected from the actors and any objects in the scene and would not return the scenery image to the camera. What about the shadow of the actor? From the viewpoint of the projector and camera, the shadow will always be hidden by the actor.

Front projection also permits a trick not possible with rear projection. This involves a second piece of retroreflective screen S2. Let the projected image be such that the edge of a doorway or the end of a wall in the scene aligns with the edge of S2. The lower circle in the diagram represents an actor who is not visible to the camera as he is behind S2. By walking from behind S2, the actor will appear to come through the doorway or from behind the wall.

After describing how he came up with his invention, Jenkins then told of other problems that he encountered. The Patent Office rejected his claims and it was necessary for him to go to Washington to meet with the patent examiner. He was able to counter each of the examiner's arguments and was granted his patents in 1955. He then tried to find someone who would be interested in using his basic idea or develop it into a commercially practical system.

In the biography of Jenkins by his daughters, there is a description of his attempts to license his basic idea to various companies including CBS, NBC and RCA, but no dates are given. In 1963, he was contacted by Sherman Fairchild, who was interested in acquiring the patents. Jenkins accepted the offer, and systems based on his patents were manufactured and sold by Fairchild Camera and Instrument Company. As expected, they found use in movies and television. But they were also used by professional photographers to provide backgrounds for advertising layouts and even wedding pictures.

In the *Analog* article, Jenkins made a connection between his invention and developing an idea for a story. There exists another statement that considered such a connection from a different direction. In his essay, "Growing Up in the Future," author Michael Swanwick said:

> The late Will Jenkins, who wrote under the name of Murray Leinster, was also an inventor. He told me once that he'd get an idea for something new and then think about it for a long time, puzzling it over, until either he could make it work or he understood why it never would. If it worked, he'd patent it. If he didn't, he'd write a science fiction story in which it did.

This statement was made without an example to support it. As we know that Jenkins had only two patents, I see a problem with Swanwick saying "If it worked, he'd patent it." It has not been possible to locate any other information that points to a story and device. If we accept this as a true and accurate statement by Jenkins, can such a story and device be found?

As I said earlier, the number of works of fiction by Jenkins is quite large. Even if we only look at his science fiction, several hundred short works and nearly fifty novels would have to be examined. What would we be looking for? We could dismiss any story device that was clearly technically impossible, such as the matter duplicator in "The Fourth Dimensional Demonstrator." We would be looking for a device that was crucial to the plot of the story and would initially appear to be technically possible. If we went back and looked at such a device again, however, it might become clear that it is not possible to construct something that really worked as described.

I obviously have not read every work of science fiction written by Jenkins. But I have identified one story that I think illustrates the statement attributed to him by Swanwick. This is the short story "Politics" that appeared in the June 1932 issue of *Amazing Stories*.

"Politics" is the story of naval warfare at a time when the United States is portrayed as being pacifist. As the story opens, the United States has just suffered a massive defeat in a battle against a Pacific Ocean enemy that is not named. (Gee, I wonder who he meant??) Only a small number of ships have survived to take part in the next and apparently final battle. As this battle approaches, the politicians in Washington are debating whether or not to accept the terms imposed by the enemy.

The Navy has determined to go down fighting rather than simply give up. One of the ships that will take part in the final battle is the super battleship U.S.S. *Minnesota*. It had not been in the previous battle as it was in port being repaired after a boiler explosion.

The *Minnesota* and the remnants of the U.S. Fleet go out for the final battle. The battle occurs close enough to the coast for the Fleet to be aided by land-based Army planes. Due to the superior targeting and fire control capabilities of the *Minnesota*, the U.S. Fleet wins the battle.

Following the battle, a message is received from Washington. Congress has decided to accept the peace terms imposed by the enemy. Consequently, the President sends the message:

> To the Senior Officer Commanding American Vessels of War in the Pacific Ocean:
>
> > Immediately on receipt of this order you will surrender all vessels under your command to the officer in command of the enemy battle fleet off our coasts.

The Captain of the *Minnesota* has the pleasure of replying:

> To the President of the United States:

> There is no longer an enemy fleet off our coasts. We have destroyed it.

The story concludes with the mood of the country shifting from pacifism to patriotism and a comment that the Army and Navy are not toys for politicians.

What was the device that made it possible for the *Minnesota* to destroy so many enemy ships? At the beginning of the story, the *Minnesota* is shown easily destroying some enemy ships following the first battle. As the naval officer who is the main character explains to another officer, this was done using new automatic rangefinders. Before I give the details from the story, I should explain how rangefinding is actually done.

In the days before radar, rangefinding was done purely by optical means. There were two basic types of rangefinders: coincidence and stereoscopic. Both types employed a tube that was perpendicular to the line of sight to the target being ranged. To get the best performance the tube should be as long as is practical. The maximum length for such tubes was about 18 feet.

The coincidence rangefinder had a single eyepiece. Optics at each end of the tube provided an image of the target. The angles of the optical elements were adjusted until the two images of the target were aligned in the view seen through the eyepiece. Consider a very narrow triangle with the target at the apex and rangefinder tube as the base. If you know the base and the angles involved, you know the range. As the target gets further away, the triangle gets narrower and the possible error increases.

The stereoscopic rangefinder had two eyepieces, each fed by the optics at the ends of the tube. To visualize this, consider it as a very wide pair of binoculars. The use of this system required a person with perfect binocular vision. Such a person would see a single object but with a sense of depth. The range was found by moving a marker internal to the optics until it coincided with the image.

Returning to "Politics," we have the description of the automatic rangefinder:

> Two telescopes, one at each end of a base-line, and mounted exactly parallel. Fitted with photoelectric cells instead of eyepieces. You swing the base-line around and they sweep the horizon. And a ship on the horizon changes the amount of light that goes through a narrow slit to the photoelectric cell. It registers the instant the first telescope hits the stern of the ship. A fraction of a second later – because the telescopes are exactly parallel – the

ship-image registers on the other cell. Both cells register exactly the same changes in current-output, but one is a fraction of a second behind the other. Knowing the rate of sweep in seconds or mils of arc, if one photoelectric cell lags behind the other one mil, and you know the base-line, you work out the distance in a hurry. . . . Those range-finders sweep their field ten times per second, ranging each way. We range the enemy ship twenty times per second and get electric impulses to read off. But better than that, we range our own shell-splashes and the target together, with the same instrument, at the same time!

Sounds quite plausible, doesn't it?

First consider the mechanical problem of his design. The two telescopes must be mounted so that they are perfectly aligned. But the process of traversing in one direction and then the other means that you have frequent reversals of direction. The whole mounting system must slam to a stop and then start in the opposite direction. This creates forces and vibrations that would affect the telescopes and their accuracy. One could increase the rigidity of the mounting system, but this would mean a heavier object to rotate back and forth. It would make more sense to continually rotate the mounting in one direction like a radar antenna.

Next consider the geometry of such a system. The situation is similar to that of a coincidence rangefinder. The greater the target distance, the smaller the rotation that is required. To see this, you can perform a simple experiment with a 3 by 5 index card and a thumbtack as shown in Figure 15. The index card represents the rangefinder with each long side being one of the telescopes. Place the card on some base with the thumbtack through the center of the card. Place a target so that it is one foot from the pivot point. Rotate the card so that one edge points directly at the target. Then rotate it so that the other edge is now pointing at the target. In this case, the required rotation is 14.36 degrees.

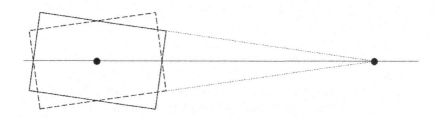

Figure 15. Rangefinder Experiment.

What happens if you increase the distance to the target to 100 feet? With the 3-inch width of the card representing a 15-foot baseline between the telescopes, a distance to the target in this experiment of 100 feet would mean a real target distance of 6,000 feet. In such a case, the required rotation would be only 0.1432 degrees. In an actual battle, the distances would be even greater than 6,000 feet and the corresponding rotation even smaller. Would the optics and the photocells be capable of giving an accurate indication based on such a very small rotation?

Let us assume that we have somehow solved these problems. There is one more very important problem to consider. The key to the victory of the *Minnesota* is the discovery that the photocells in the rangefinder are sensitive to infrared light. The main character observes that when you look at the Sun through a smoke screen it appears red. The question is, if all of the visible light is blocked by smoke, will the infrared light still get through? The rangefinder is tested and it is discovered that it will work through a smoke screen. In the final battle, both the U.S. Fleet and the enemy Fleet form smoke screens for their protection. The *Minnesota* has no trouble at all locating the enemy ships through both smoke screens and destroying them with accurate gunfire.

But would this really work? If we assume that the smoke screen was composed of hot gases from the stack of the ship, it seemed to me that you would not be able to use infrared to see a colder object behind it. When I was back at Johns Hopkins University for a reunion, I took the opportunity to get an answer to my question from a member of the faculty. I described the story and my question to Dr. Charbel Rizk, who is an Associate Research Professor in the Department of Electrical and Computer Engineering. He agreed with my observation that you could not see a colder object – the ship – behind a smoke screen of hot gases. Dr. Rizk did point out, however, that one hot part of the ship would be the stack itself. He then suggested that it might be possible with modern sensors and processing of the data to detect a solitary hot spot such as the stack, but it would not have been possible with the infrared technology of the 1930s.

The automatic infrared rangefinders are not possible for several reasons. Does this mean that I am correct in my selection of "Politics"? We will probably never know. If someone out there wishes to look at more of his stories to find plausible sounding but impossible devices, let me know what you find out. I think, however, that "Politics" demonstrates the approach attributed to Jenkins. We can imagine him coming up with the rangefinder idea and then finding it was just not possible. He then presented it in the story in a way that would convince most readers that it would work.

This is all I wish to say about Will Jenkins and inventions. But I would like to conclude this chapter by presenting a technical description from one of his stories. In the story, a computer is called a "logic." The main character is a serviceman for the company that manufactures logics and he describes how they are used:

> You know the logics setup. You got a logic in your house. It looks like a vision receiver used to, only it's got keys instead of dials and you punch the keys for what you wanna get. It's hooked in to the tank, which has the Carson Circuit all fixed up with relays. Say you punch in "Station SNAFU" on your logic. Relays in the tank take over an' whatever vision-program SNAFU is telecastin' comes on your logic's screen. Or you punch "Sally Hancock's Phone" an' the screen blinks an' sputters you're hooked up with the logic in her house an' if somebody answers you got a vision-phone connection. But besides that, if you punch for the weather forecast or who won today's race at Hialeah or who was the mistress of the White House durin' Garfield's administration or what is PDQ and R sellin' for today, that comes up on the screen too. The relays in the tank do it. The tank is a big buildin' full of all the facts in creation an' all the recorded telecasts that ever was made – an' it's hooked in with all the other tanks all over the country – an' anything you wanna know or see or hear, you punch for it an' you get it.

I think that you will agree that this is a fair description of some of the services that one now obtains from the Internet. What makes it such an amazing description is that it is from the story "A Logic Named Joe" that appeared in *Astounding Science-Fiction* in March 1946. The story appeared as by Will F. Jenkins because he had another story in the same issue as by Murray Leinster.

One of the logics that comes off the assembly line is different in some very subtle way. This difference is not detected in testing so the logic is placed in service. Once it is part of the larger system, it affects the circuits which normally censor the type of information provided to users. One man is told of an undetectable way to murder his blonde wife. A teenager is told how to create almost perfect counterfeit money. A banker learns how his own bank can be robbed. The number of such incidents grows. The logic serviceman, nicknamed Ducky, manages to track down the logic responsible, which he calls Joe. He removes it from service and tells the company that it was destroyed when he fell while carrying it. He actually places Joe, unpowered, on the shelf in his cellar. By doing so, Ducky claims he has saved civilization. As the story ends, however, Ducky is trying to decide whether he should leave Joe turned off or power it up for some personal benefit.

One question that might be asked regarding "A Logic Named Joe" is whether anyone later responsible for the development of the Internet was aware of the story. A second, more interesting question is where Jenkins got the idea for the way the logics would be used by people to communicate and retrieve information.

Regarding that second question, I wonder if Jenkins had read "As We May Think" by Vannevar Bush, which appeared in *The Atlantic Monthly* in July 1945. At least the timing is right for the creation of "A Logic Named Joe." In the article, Bush describes a hypothetical device that he calls a "memex." Although the article says that the choice of the name was random, it could be based on *memory* and *index* or *memory* and *extender*.

The memex would be a means of supplementing and aiding a person's memory. Envisioned in a pre-digital age, books and documents would be stored by microphotography. The user would be able to store, access and view all types of such material. In addition, the memex would enable the user to create "trails" between items; what we now call links. It is this feature of the memex that is seen as an inspiration for hypertext.

This question of the connection between the memex and "A Logic Named Joe" is simply another for which we may never have an answer. But it enables me to close this chapter with one more thing for you to think about. There are many sources that may inspire an inventor. If we accept that science fiction can, as I hope I have demonstrated, serve as the inspiration for the development of an invention, what can we say about the sources of inspiration for the story idea that leads to the invention?

10

SUMMARY

In Chapter 2, I presented the S-E chart as a way to organize the various cases where an invention may or may not have been inspired by a work of science fiction. Since Chapters 3 through 8 were concerned with such cases, the next logical step would be to see how each of those cases might be placed on the chart. For the discussion that follows, please refer to Figure 16.

I will begin with the lower right region of the chart, which is the area of HIGH evidence FOR inspiration and of LOW similarity. Only one item has been placed there: Chain Reaction. The marker is right on the line that indicates absolute certainty. Even though there is evidence that there were several factors that influenced Szilard, we know from his own statements that one of them was *The World Set Free*.

Now consider the vertical position of the marker. There was absolutely nothing in *The World Set Free* that could have pointed to a chain reaction as the key to nuclear energy. The existence of a subatomic particle such as the neutron was not even suspected at the time that the story was written. The only common factor between story and invention is the release of energy. We must also consider how the energy release was to occur. If we look at the way that the bombs and their operation were described by Wells, there is very little resemblance to what could actually result from a chain reaction. Therefore, I am fairly confident in placing it quite low on the vertical line.

Now move to the upper right region of the chart, which is the area of HIGH evidence FOR inspiration and of HIGH similarity. I have placed three items there: Dracone, Denisyuk Holography and Radioactive Dust.

Figure 16. Placement of cases.

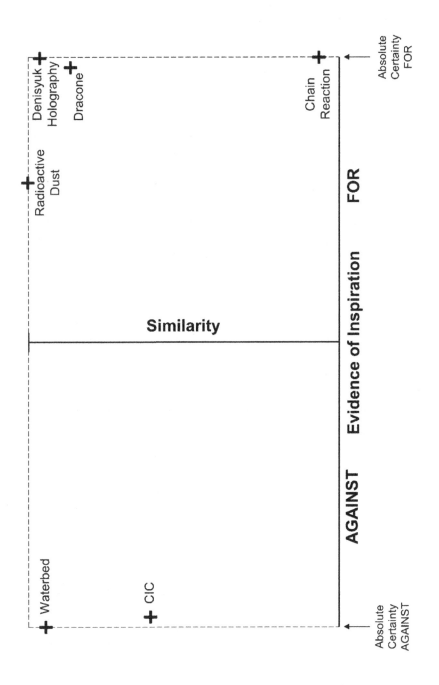

Absolute
Certainty
FOR

Denisyuk
Holography

Dracone

Chain
Reaction

Radioactive
Dust

FOR

Similarity

Evidence of Inspiration

AGAINST

Waterbed

CIC

Absolute
Certainty
AGAINST

Of the three, the position of Dracone in this region is well established. With all of the evidence that I have been able to find to support inspiration by *Under Pressure*, I still do not have a direct statement by Hawthorne. This means that I cannot place the marker directly on the vertical line indicating certainty. I have it very close to the line because the evidence is so good.

Why is the marker for the Dracone not on the top horizontal line? If it was on the line, it would mean an exact match between the slug of Herbert's story and the Dracone. Although they are very close in appearance and function, remember that the slug had to have the features to permit it to operate submerged, while the Dracone operated only on the surface. This difference means that the marker must be a slight distance below the horizontal line.

Now let us look at Denisyuk Holography. We have a definite statement of influence by a work of science fiction, namely Yefremov's "Star Ships." This places the marker on the right vertical line. I had originally equated similarity with the ability to link an invention to a story. Consider the case of *The World Set Free*. In the absence of a statement by Szilard, would you have been inclined to link that story to the Chain Reaction? For the same reason, I had initially placed Denisyuk Holography in the lower right region of the chart, in close proximity to the Chain Reaction.

The more that I thought about it, however, the more I felt that it should be moved higher. All that we have in "Star Ships" for the basis of comparison is the image of the alien in the artifact. According to the story, the image simply appears when viewed in normal white light without the need for special equipment. The same is true of a Denisyuk hologram. The only difference seems to be in the color of the image. It is implied, rather than stated, that the image in the alien artifact appears in its natural colors. You will recall from in Chapter 4 that the process of recreating the image from the hologram results it in being monochrome. For this degree of similarity, I have moved Denisyuk Holography very high on the vertical line.

What do we do with the case of Radioactive Dust? As far as similarity is concerned, the fictional concept in Heinlein's story and that proposed in the Committee report are identical. Both described the use of radioactive material to be dropped on enemy territory. We are able to place the marker on the top horizontal line.

The problem here is with regard to the evidence. Chapter 6 was concluded with no final resolution of the question. If we were to accept that the National Academy Committee was influenced either directly by the Heinlein story or indirectly through Robert Cornog, the marker should be somewhere on the right side of the chart, its current location reflecting the lack of definite proof. That is *my* stated position. Someone else may assert that it is more likely that the Briggs Committee was the source of the idea, but again with no proof of that assertion. In that case, it would be placed on the left side of the chart, some distance from the left axis.

If evidence could be found to establish that there was an influence by the story, we then slide the marker all the way to the right. If, on the other hand, it is conclusively determined that the development of the concept was independent of the story, we then slide it all the way to the left. It's my chart and my call, so for now it stays where it is.

The upper left region of the chart is the area of HIGH evidence AGAINST inspiration and of HIGH similarity. The Waterbed clearly belongs on the left vertical line, as we have the definite statement by Charlie Hall that he was not aware of the work of Heinlein until after he had created the waterbed. As was explained in Chapter 7, there are some differences between the fictional and real waterbeds, so the marker is a short distance from the top line.

Finally, there is the Combat Information Center (CIC). I have presented much evidence to show that it was not influenced by the writing of Doc Smith as had been claimed. For that reason, it should be placed very near but not on the vertical line. There are substantial differences between the CIC and the tank in Smith's *Directrix*. This places the marker some distance down on the graph in terms of similarity.

I am confident of the general placement of five of the six items. Radioactive Dust is the only case where the final placement of the marker requires the discovery of additional evidence.

The strongest statement that I can make about my research and its results is that the sample size is just too damned small. It is too small to come to any definite conclusions about the role of science fiction in the process of invention. But I am able to speculate and to ask some questions.

Is there any common factor among the stories in which the source of inspiration was found to occur? Both *The World Set Free* (Chain Reaction) and "Solution Unsatisfactory" (Radioactive Dust) involved warfare. *Under Pressure* (Dracone) was a story of conflict between the Eastern and Western Powers involving submarine warfare. We could interpret "Star Ships" (Denisyuk Holography) either as a story of paleontological exploration or alien visitation. In doing so, we should not ignore the fact that the discovery of the evidence of the alien visit and the artifact displaying the alien image was only possible because of their violent acts against the dinosaurs.

What happens when we also look at the two cases that were shown not to be inspired by science fiction? *Gray Lensman* (CIC) was a story of interstellar warfare. The group of stories of Robert Heinlein that includes *Stranger in a Strange Land* (Waterbed) appear to be the exception as there is no common factor of violence or warfare among the stories.

Does this mean that we are more likely than not to find cases of inspiration in science fiction stories that feature violence and warfare?

What can we say about the men who were inspired? Consider the case of just one invention: the Dracone. How many people read *Under Pressure* when it was first published? Of those, how many asked themselves if it would be possible to actually build something like the slug in the story? If someone other than William Hawthorne had tried to build something like the Dracone and had encountered the problems such as snaking and tail flick, would they have had the education, knowledge and experience that he was able to use to solve these and other problems to make the Dracone a success?

Generalizing from the example of the Dracone, the inspiration of inventions would seem to depend more on the people who are being inspired than the stories that are doing the inspiring. It has been said that many of the readers of science fiction are engineers and scientists. Any possible sources of inspiration in those stories are being presented to just those people who are both likely to respond to the inspiration and to have the necessary knowledge and skills to make use of the inspiration.

The only way to answer some of the questions that I have posed and hopefully obtain some definite answers is to find more cases of inspiration by science fiction. When should we look for such cases? You will notice that I said **when** and not **where**. This is a bit of speculation on my part. Look at the cases I have investigated and the year when the inspiration occurred, whether it was from science fiction or not:

Chain Reaction	1933
CIC	1940
Radioactive Dust	1941
Dracone	1956
Denisyuk Holography	1958
Waterbed	1968

The point I wish to make is that there is nothing in my sample later than the 1960s. And the latest is one of the cases where there was no inspiration by science fiction.

Are we now at a time when it is not likely that we will encounter cases of inspiration from current works of science fiction? Please note that I am not saying that it is no longer possible for such inspiration to occur. I am simply saying that if we wish to find more such cases, we should be looking at older inventions and works of science fiction. I suggest that the greater number will be found in the period roughly from the 1930s to the 1990s, as opposed to the 1990s or later.

Assume that you are someone in the 1930s with an interest in science and technology. You might be very young and still in school or you might be a bit older and out in the workplace. Are concepts such as space travel or power from the atom likely to be encountered in most schools or in the technical literature? No. The source of such ideas for most people would have been in the pages of the much-maligned works of science fiction. ("Why do you read such trash?" asked the teacher.)

Even after the atomic bombs were used in World War II and we had the beginning of the space age in the mid-1950s, science fiction still seemed to be the best place to encounter similar outrageous concepts for the first time. Concepts that could serve as the inspiration for an invention.

And possibly encounter them at an early age. Where did I first come across the concept of something orbiting the earth at just the right speed that it would remain over a spot on the planet? Or the idea of moving between the planets in paths that took a long time but were economical in the amount of energy (fuel) required? It occurred when I was in the third grade in 1959, but not in a classroom. It was in the pages of Heinlein's juvenile novel *Space Cadet*. Incidentally, this novel also contained one of Heinlein's mentions of a portable telephone. It should not be forgotten that this book was first published in 1948.

Where is someone most likely to encounter all sorts of weird and highly speculative ideas today? Including ideas that could inspire an invention. I would say on the Internet. That is why I place the cut-off point sometime in the 1990s.

My suggestion does create a problem. As in any type of historical research, the older the case is, the harder it will be to determine the facts. Look at the six cases that I investigated. The only case where I was able to get the facts directly from the person involved was Charlie Hall and the Waterbed.

Or is the basis of my speculation just another consequence of the small sample size?

What about Chapter 9 and the science fiction authors who were also inventors? I will continue to look for such authors. I will also look at more of the stories by Will Jenkins/Murray Leinster to see if I can find another one that seems, like "Politics," to be based on the idea for an invention that just could not be reduced to practice.

I will obviously keep looking to find and investigate more cases of inspiration by science fiction. I expect to hear from people who will ask, "Do you know about X?" or "Why didn't you include Y?" I would love to be able to create *Out of This World Ideas 2.0* with a whole bunch of new cases.

I want to see a future version of the S-E chart populated with many new cases. I do not want to see a lot of cases on the far left, which indicates no inspiration by science fiction. Likewise, I do not want to see a lot of cases in the middle along the Similarity axis, which means that there is no evidence one way or the other.

Before you go to my website at **www.emwysocki.com** and send me a message, take a few minutes to think about the invention and story that you are going to suggest to me. Ask yourself some questions: "Am I basing this suggestion solely on similarity of appearance or function?" "Do I know when the invention was made?" "Do I know when the story first appeared?" "Do I know anything at all about the inventor?" "Did the inventor ever say where the idea came from?" I think you get the general idea. After you have thought about it a bit and still feel that you have a good case to present, just let me know. I cannot guarantee that I will respond to every message, but I will try. If you are the first person to provide me with a new case of inspiration by science fiction that I am able to use in a future book, I will definitely give you credit as the source.

NOTES

Introduction

1   Speculations of science fiction: Heinlein, "Virtues", 24-26.

1   List of science fiction authors: Ibid., 28.

1   I had a completely imaginary electronics device in a story published in 1939. A classmate of mine, then directing such research, took it to his civilian chief engineer and asked if it could possibly be done. The researcher replied, "Mmm ... no, I don't think so— uh, wait a minute . . . well, yes, maybe. We'll try."

The bread-boarded first model was being tried out aboard ship before the next installment of my story hit the newsstands. The final development of this gadget was in use all during World War II. I wasn't predicting anything and had no reason to think that it would work; I was just dreaming up a gadget to fill a need in a story, sticking as close to fact and possibility as I could.   Ibid., 28-29.

2   Described in chapters of first book: Wysocki, *Mystery*, 128-44.

Chapter 1

5   Bailey biographical details: *Pilgrims*, book jacket.

6   "A piece of scientific fiction": Ibid., 10.

6   "It would be interesting": Ibid., 261.

6   "Even though": Ibid., 262.

7   Websites: "10 inventions"; Dufault; Strauss.

7 "scientists and explorers": Gunn, 210.

7 Smithsonian article: Strauss.

8 Diving chamber: Lake, 12.

8 "In 1995": Dufault.

9 History of GPS: Parkinson.

10 Warp drive: Alcubierre.

10 Bell Labs: Gertner, 281-82.

11 Cooper regarding inspiration: *Scene World Magazine.*

12 Tricorder XPrize objectives: "Qualcomm", 3-5.

12 XPrize conditions: Ibid., 5-6, 22-28.

14 Taser inspiration: Weber.

Chapter 3

19 Demonstration in Mediterranean: Cromie, Chapter XI.

19 Becquerel discovers radioactivity: Rhodes, 41-42.

19 Claim that radioactivity inspired Cromie: Franklin, 50.

20 "A quantity of matter": Preston, 115.

20 "If you will consult": Cromie, Chapter II.

21 Rutherford, alpha, beta: Rhodes, 42.

21 Villard, gamma: Ibid., 42.

21 Alpha particle demonstration: Ibid., 45.

22 "This bottle contains": Soddy, 229.

22 "to increase the natural rate": Ibid., 230.

23 "if it were possible": Ibid., 230.

23 Work on *The World Set Free*: Smith, *H. G. Wells*, 83.

24 "I've suddenly broken out": Ibid., 83-84.

24   Rufus lecture: Wells, 23-29.

24   Holsten and other processes: Ibid., 30-41.

24   Effects on society: Ibid., 44-45.

25   "Those used by the allies": Ibid., 100-01.

25   Birth of Szilard: Lanouette, 12.

25   Change of family name: Ibid., 13.

26   Unconventional math solutions: Ibid., 24-25.

26   Entry in to practical school: Ibid., 31.

26   War and University: Ibid., 36-37.

26   Fourth Mountain-Artillery Regiment: Ibid., 39.

26   Influenza: Ibid., 40-42.

26   Successive Hungarian governments: Ibid., 43-49.

26   Unable to study at Technical University: Ibid., 49.

27   Technische Hochschule: Ibid., 52, 56.

27   Switch to Friedrich Wilhelm University: Ibid., 56.

27   Ph.D. Thesis: Ibid., 58-60.

28   Various ideas: Ibid., 83-86, 94-95, 101-02.

28   Departure from Germany: Ibid., 114-16.

29   "This just goes to show": Ibid., 116.

29   Plum-pudding model: Rhodes, 40.

29   Gold foils: Ibid., 48-50.

30   Problems with structure of nucleus: Ibid., 154-55.

30   Neutron proposed: Ibid., 153.

30   Chadwick and neutron: Ibid., 159-64.

31   Szilard in London: Lanouette, 118-27.

31   Rutherford talk: Ibid., 132-33.

31   Reading *The World Set Free*: Weart, 16.

31   Mandl: Ibid., 16-17.

31   "because only through": Ibid., 17.

31   Date of walk: Lanouette, 508 Note 4.

31   "if we could find": Ibid., 133.

32   Beryllium: Ibid., 137-38.

33   Indium: Ibid., 153.

33   Research with Chalmers: Ibid., 146-47.

33   Patent to Admiralty: Ibid., 156, 158.

33   Artificial radioactive isotopes: Rhodes, 200-02.

33   Fermi: Ibid., 209-13, 216-18.

34   Hahn and Strassmann: Ibid., 252-55.

34   Meitner and Frisch: Ibid., 257-60.

Chapter 4

35   Yefremov childhood: Shelokhonov.

35   Sixth Army: Yefremov, *Stories*, 7.

36   Sushkin: Ibid., 7-8.

36   Subsequent career: Ibid., 8-9.

37   "Against the bluish black slab": Ibid., 28.

39   "The two scientists": Ibid., 259.

39   Gabor birth and family: Allibone, 107.

40   Desire to become engineer: Ibid., 108.

40   University and military: Ibid., 110.

40   Technische Hochschule: Ibid., 110.

40 "There were far too many": Ibid., 110.

40 Thesis research: Ibid., 111.

41 "he had already made": Ibid., 113.

41 Knoll and Ruska: Freundlich, 185.

43 "Why not take": Gabor, 13.

44 Denisyuk's parents: Stafeev, 114.

44 Yuri with grandmother: Ibid., 44.

45 Mother remarries: Ibid., 46, 115.

45 Residence in Leningrad: Ibid., 46.

45 Influences on Yuri: Ibid., 47, 115.

45 Verevkino: Ibid., 49, 115-16.

45 Siege and evacuation: Ibid., 50, 116.

45 Education in Kolomna: Ibid., 52, 116.

46 Leningrad, LIFMO: Ibid., 53-56, 64, 116-18.

46 State Optical Institute: Ibid., 118-19.

46 "very dull work": Johnston, "Yuri Denisyuk", 8.

47 Claim about "Shadows from the Past": Yefremov, "From the Author".

47 "At the time": Denisyuk, 425.

47 "A thrill pierced": Ibid., 425.

47 "The two scientists": Yefremov, *Stories*, 259.

48 Wave field: Denisyuk, 425.

49 Approach: Ibid., 426.

51 Publication: Johnston, "Yuri Denisyuk", 10.

51 Enemies: Denisyuk, 428.

51 Leith background: Johnston, "Emmett Leith", 2.

51   SAR: Stimson, 399-410.

52   Optical processing: Leith, 432.

53   "A line of optical scientists": "Emmett Leith" ECE.

Chapter 5

55   1955 Oil figures: Pierre, 45.

56   Hawthorne early life: Greitzer, 133.

56   Cambridge: Newland.

56   MIT: Chu; Greitzer, 134.

57   Sc.D., Marriage: Greitzer, 134.

57   Whittle early life: Pavelec, 39-40.

57   RAF: Ibid., 40-43.

57   Officer Engineering Course, Cambridge: Ibid., 43.

58   Vaporized Fuel: Lloyd, 5.

58   Lubbock: Pavelec, 59.

59   "With several others": Hawthorne, "History of Aircraft Gas Turbine", 99-100.

59   First flights: Pavelec, 22, 62.

60   Unmixedness: Beer, 143.

60   Secondary flow: Greitzer, 135.

60   Cambridge, Thermodynamics: Newland.

60   MIT Visiting Professor: Greitzer, 135.

60   Interest in science fiction: Ibid., 138.

61   Working on *Under Pressure*: Herbert, *Dreamer*, 73, 83.

61   Senator Cordon: Ibid., 87-99.

61   Sale to *Astounding*: Ibid., 106.

62   Sale to Doubleday: Ibid., 106.

61   *Dragon in the Sea* title: Ibid., 113.

62   "A slug will carry": Herbert, "Under Pressure (Part 1)", 10.

63   "Full slug": Herbert, "Under Pressure (Part 3)", 86.

64   "The six hundred feet": Herbert, "Under Pressure (Part 1)", 48.

65   Conversation with Shaw: Hawthorne, "Development of Dracone", 53.

65   "I do not remember": Hawthorne, "Sausages", 7.

65   First calculation: Hawthorne, "Development of Dracone", 53.

66   Snaking: Ibid., 54.

67   Name of dracone: Ibid., 55.

67   Draconella, draconeel: Ibid., 55.

67   Surplus of tankers: Ibid., 57.

69   Tail flick: Hawthorne, "The Dracone Project", 44.

69   Fixes for snaking: Hawthorne, "Development of Dracone", 65-67.

69   Fixes for tail flick: Hawthorne, "The Dracone Project", 44-45.

69   Model testing: Ibid., 63.

70   Barge models: "The Dracone Barge".

71   "Dad consulted a number": Herbert, *Dreamer*, 200.

71   Hawthorne career, awards: Greitzer, 136-37.

71   "flexible undersea oil barge": O'Reilly, 35.

71   "flexible underwater barge": Herbert, *Dreamer*, 200.

71   "flexible submarine tanker": Clarke, 50.

72   "string of submersible oil-barges": Ibid., 50.

72   "I got the idea": Ibid., 50.

72   "During the early part": Hawthorne, "Dracones", 13.

Chapter 6

75 Lawrence early life: Hiltzik, 29.

75 St. Olaf: Ibid., 32.

75 USD: Ibid., 33.

76 University of Minnesota: Ibid., 33-36.

76 Master's Thesis: Alvarez, "Lawrence", 288.

76 Ph.D. dissertation: Ibid., 288.

76 Move to Berkeley: Hiltzik, 43.

77 High voltages: Heilbron, 50, 53, 60.

78 Work by Lawrence and Livingston: Ibid., 89.

78 80,000 volts: Ibid., 95.

78 Electric fields as lenses: Rhodes, 148.

78 1.2 MeV: Heilbron, 100.

79 Growth in cyclotron size: Ibid., 130-31, 269, 483.

79 Cornog early life: Steiner, 1.

79 Mechanical Engineering: Ibid., 3.

79 Bureau of Reclamation: Ibid., 4, 7.

79 Robert Heinlein: Ibid., 89-90.

80 Berkeley: Ibid., 9-10.

80 Radiosodium: Heilbron, 188.

80 ^{3}H and ^{3}He mystery: Ibid., 368-370.

81 Alvarez at Berkeley: Alvarez. "Physicist", Chapter 2.

81 Detection of ^{3}He: Ibid., Chapter 3; Heilbron, 370-72.

82 ^{3}H half-life: Heilbron, 372.

82 Campbell early life: Berger, 15.

83   MIT, Duke: Ibid., 15-19.

83   Editor of *Astounding*: Ibid., 33.

83   "But you can be certain: Campbell, "Fantastic Fiction", 21.

84   Campbell letter 01/15/40: CORR218-1, 37.

84   Heinlein letter 01/20/40: Ibid., 40.

84   Campbell reply: Ibid., 43-44.

85   At the end of January: Ibid., 47.

85   Story submitted: Ibid., 52.

85   "All U-235 will do": McCann, "Shhhhh", 113.

86   "Story goes, the Romans": Ibid., 113.

86   "Buildings and walls": Ridley, 144.

87   "I've just reread": CORR218-1, 158.

87   Story outline letter: Ibid., 162-63.

87   Heinlein letter 12/17/40: Ibid., 164.

88   Story submission 12/24/40: Ibid., 165.

88   Campbell reaction: Ibid., 170.

88   Heinlein reply to reaction: Ibid., 177.

88   Discussion of changes: Ibid., 184.

89   Lawrence Nobel Prize: Heilbron, 492; Hiltzik, 188.

89   Letter to Roosevelt: Hewlett, 16-17.

89   Briggs Committee: Ibid., 19-20.

89   Changes to Committee: Ibid., 25.

90   Problems with Briggs Committee: Ibid., 35.

90   Formation of National Academy Committee: Ibid., 36-37.

90   Proposed military applications: May 17 NAS Report, 2.

91   Occurrence of two events: Franklin, 142; Gifford, 173-74.

91   "Some thought": Compton, 47.

91   "radiation bombs": Hewlett, 37.

92   "Well, there were at one time": Steiner, 120.

Chapter 7

93   Heinlein early life: Patterson, Volume 1, 18-27.

93   Reading: Ibid., 30-32, 39.

94   Academy appointment limits: Chisholm, 619.

94   Reed appointment: Patterson, Volume 1, 42.

94   Fencing: Ibid., 53.

94   Final year: Ibid., 99-109.

94   First marriage: Ibid., 113.

94   Divorce: Ibid., 131.

95   Training at Ford Instrument: Ibid., 121-25.

95   Fleet Problem XII: Wadle, 66-69.

95   Fleet Problem, Heinlein and Scoles: Patterson, Volume I, 135-36.

95   Panama: Heinlein, "Happy Days Ahead", 517-18.

96   Marriage to Leslyn: Patterson, Volume 1, 144-52.

96   Promotion to Lieutenant, j.g.: Ibid., 155.

96   Transfer to *Roper*: Ibid., 158.

96   Diagnosis of TB: Ibid., 159.

96   Problems at Fitzsimmons: Ibid., 164-66.

97   "Some years later": Heinlein, "Happy Days Ahead", 518.

97   Retirement: Patterson, Volume 1, 167, 170.

97   Advanced degree problems: Ibid., 171.

97 California politics: Ibid., 173-213.

97 "Life-Line": Ibid., 229-31.

97 "How long has this": Ibid., 231.

98 "The water rose gently": MacDonald, "Beyond", 17.

98 "The deceleration tanks": MacDonald, "Waldo", 16.

99 "The tank was not": Ibid., 33.

99 "Each tank was like": Heinlein, "Sky Lift", 119.

99 "Against one bulkhead": Heinlein, *Double Star*, 29.

100 "transferred into": Heinlein, *Stranger*, 11.

100 "The patient floated": Ibid., 14.

100 "Sure, you're weak": Ibid., 17.

100 "He switched on": Ibid., 47.

100 "A patient that old": Ibid., 58.

101 "it consists of": Cooper, 709-10.

101 Problem with Arnott design: Webster, 309-11.

101 "as the inventor": "The Late William Hooper", 416.

The biographical material on Charles Prior Hall (including statements by Mr. Hall) as presented on pages 102-104, 105-106 and 111, is taken from a series of emails received from Mr. Hall on March 18, 2018; May 10, 2018; June 5, 2018 and June 22, 2018. Additional material is taken from emails received from Darlene Tong on March 28, 2018; March 29, 2018 and April 5, 2018.

106 "Some joker tried": Heinlein, "Happy Days Ahead", 516-17.

107 "It was not the first": Ibid., 517.

107 Share Water Bed: Patterson, Volume 2, 326, 596 Note 48.

107 "I designed the water bed": Heinlein, "Happy Days Ahead", 517.

108 "A person shall be": "35 U.S.C".

108 Donald Duck: "The 'Donald Duck as Prior art' case".

109 PHOSITA: Brean, 7.

Chapter 8

113 Hertz: Gebhard, 5.

115 Western Electric vacuum tube: Howeth, Chapter XVII, Sec. 8.

116 Radio on ships: Wolters, *Information*, 68-70.

116 Fleet Problem IX: Ibid.,130-31.

117 Improved radio procedures: Ibid.,145, 147.

118 Early radar: Gebhard, 173-79.

118 CXZ and XAF: Wolters, *Information*, 180-81.

119 CXAM and CXAM-1: Ibid., 183, 186.

120 Tank dimensions: Smith, "Gray Lensman", 138.

122 "Red lights": Ibid., 138.

122 "If, as I believe": Ibid.,146.

123 *California*: Wolters, Dissertation, 222-23.

123 *Yorktown*: Ibid., 225-26.

124 PPI: Boslaugh, 15, 23-44.

124 IFF: Gebhard, 251-55.

124 "Following graduation": Laning Naval Biography.

125 General Line: Wysocki, *Mystery*, 81-82.

125 Laning's Commanding Officer: Tisdale Naval Biography.

128 "His development": Laning Service Record.

128 "For info, I have been": CORR305-1945, 77-78.

129 "The development of": *CIC Handbook*.

130 "CIC was introduced": Campbell letter to Smith.

131 Claims about Smith: Brake and Hook, 96-97.

Chapter 9

133 Gernsback early life: Ashley, 16-18.

133 Businesses: Ibid., 19-20.

134 "to teach the young": Ibid., 20.

134 Patents: Kraeuter, 174-75.

134 Magazines: Ashley, 22, 31-3, 53, 77, 104, 205.

134 Bankruptcy: Ibid., 132-35.

134 *Ralph 124C41+*: Ibid., 27-31.

135 hypnobioscope: Ibid., 29.

136 Quantum dots: McCarthy, 28-33.

136 Color TV displays: Luo, 28-33, 52-53.

137 Leinster early Life: Stallings, 17-21.

137 Start as writer: Ibid., 25-29.

138 World War I: Ibid., 29.

138 Types of stories: Ibid., 195-214.

138 Scoles Letter, January 1942: ANNA201a-09, 25-26.

138 "If I understand": ANNA201a-08, 293-94.

139 Leinster suggestions: CORR218-3, 161.

139 OWI devices: Stallings, 90-91.

139 Letter to Heinlein, July 1945: CORR220-1, 61.

140 Periscope wake: Resnick, 104-05.

140 Anti-kamikaze idea: Ibid., 103-04.

140 "Did you send": CORR220-2, 70.

140 1963 letter: Barrett, 202.

141 "But I was a science-fiction writer": Jenkins, "Applied" 110.

143 Patent problems: Ibid., 121-22.

143 Licensing and sale: Stallings, 140-42.

143 "The late Will Jenkins.": Swanwick.

144 "To the Senior Officer": Leinster, 279.

145 Rangefinding: Friedman, 22-28.

145 "Two telescopes": Leinster, 273.

148 "You know the logics setup": Jenkins, "Logic", 140.

BIBLIOGRAPHY

Archived Material, Letters and Other Special Sources

Campbell, John W. Jr. Letter to E. E. "Doc" Smith, June 11, 1947.

Churchill Archives Centre, The Papers of Sir William Hawthorne, HATN.

"The Dracone Project." *Journal of the Cambridge University Engineering Society* 37 (1967): 40-46, HATN 4/3/11 file 1.

"Dracones." (June 1960): 1-17, HATN 4/3/11 file 3.

"Sausages from High Table: A piece of practical research." *Trinity Review* (Michaelmas 1957): 7-9, HATN 4/4/3 file 9.

Heinlein Archives: ANNA201a-08, ANNA201a-09, CORR218-1, CORR218-3, CORR220-1, CORR220-2, CORR305-1945.

Martin Cooper Interview, conducted by Joerg Droege of *Scene World Magazine*. https://youtube.com/watch?v=B6OKTJMavtw.

National Academy of Sciences Archives

Minutes of the Advisory Committee of the National Academy on Uranium Disintegration, April 30, 1941.

Minutes of the Advisory Committee of the National Academy on Uranium Disintegration, May 5, 1941.

Report of National Academy Science Committee on Atomic Fission, May 17, 1941.

Naval Biography of Caleb Barrett Laning, RADM USN (Ret.)

Naval Biography of Mahlon Street Tisdale, VADM USN (Ret.)

Robert Cornog Oral History Interview, conducted by Arthur Steiner. Archived at Bancroft Library at University of California at Berkeley.

Service Record of Caleb Barrett Laning, RADM USN (Ret.)

Articles and Stories

"10 inventions that began life as science fiction." https://www.theneweconomy.com/technology/10-inventions-that-began-life-as-science-fiction (accessed June 1, 2015).

"35 U.S.C. 102 (Pre-AIA): Conditions for Patentability; Novelty and Loss of Right to Patent." https://www.bitlaw.com/source/35usc/102_(pre-AIA).html (accessed June 20, 2018).

Alcubierre, Miguel. "The Warp Drive: Hyper-Fast Travel within General Relativity." *Classical and Quantum Gravity* 11, no. 5 (May 1994): L73-L77.

Allibone, T. E. "Dennis Gabor, 5 June 1900 – 9 February 1979." *Biographical Memoirs of Fellows of the Royal Society* 26 (November 1, 1980): 106-47.

Alvarez, Luis W. "Ernest Orlando Lawrence (1901 – 1988)." *Biographical Memoirs of the National Academy of Sciences* 41 (1970): 251-94.

Barrett, Thomas M. "Heart of a Serpent? The Cold War Science Fiction of Murray Leinster." *Science Fiction Studies* 39, no. 2 (July 2012): 195-220.

Beer, Janos M., Jack B. Howard, John P. Longwell and Adel F. Sarofim. "Hoyt C. Hottel (1903 – 1998)." *Memorial Tributes: National Academy of Engineering* 10 (2002): 140-45.

Brean, Daniel H. "Keeping Time Machines and Teleporters in the Public Domain: Fiction as Prior Art for Patent Examination." *Journal of Technology Law and Policy* 7 (Spring 2007): 1-37. http://tlp.law.pitt.edu/ojs/index.php/tlp/article/view/26/26 (accessed June 15, 2017).

Campbell, John W. Jr. "Fantastic Fiction." *Astounding Science-Fiction*, June 1938, 21.

Cooper, Samuel. "Lectures on the Principles, Practice, & Operations of Surgery." *The London Medical and Surgical Journal* 2, no. 49 (January 5, 1833): 709-10.

Chu, Jennifer. "Sir William R. Hawthorne, former professor of mechanical engineering, dies at 98." MIT News, September 22, 2011. http://news.mit.edu/2011/obit-hawthorne-0922 (accessed March 3, 2018).

Denisyuk, Yuri N. "My Way in Holography." *Leonardo* 25, no. 5 (October 1992): 425-430.

"The 'Donald Duck as prior art' case." http://www.iusmentis.com/patents/priorart/donaldduck/ (accessed November 10, 2017).

"The Dracone Barge." http://trelleborg.com.au/wp-content/uploads/2011/12/Barge-leaflet.pdf (accessed January 20, 2018).

Dufault, Ashley. "10 Inventions Inspired by Science Fiction." http://www.toptenz.net/10-inventions-inspired-science-fiction.php (accessed December 24, 2017).

"Emmett Leith: Inventor of Practical Holography." http://ece.umich.edu/bicentennial/stories/emmett-leith.html (accessed June 20, 2018).

Freundlich, Martin M. "Origin of the Electron Microscope." *Science* 142, no. 3589 (October 11, 1963): 185-88.

Gabor, Dennis. "Holography, 1948-1971" In *Nobel Lectures in Physics (1971-1980)*, edited by Stig Lundqvist, 11-44. Singapore: World Scientific, 1992.

Greitzer, Edward M. and John H. Horlock. "Sir William Rede Hawthorne (1913-2011)." *Memorial Tributes: National Academy of Engineering 17 (2013)*:132-38.

Gunn, James. "Science Fiction and the Future." In *Inside Science Fiction*, 209-13. Lanham MD: Scarecrow Press, 2006.

Hawthorne, W. R. "The Early Development of the Dracone Flexible Barge." *Proceedings of the Institution of Mechanical Engineers* 175, no. 1 (June 1961): 52-83.

---. "The Early History of the Aircraft Gas Turbine in Britain." *Notes and Records of the Royal Society of London* 45, no. 1 (January 1991): 79-108.

Heinlein, Robert A. "Science Fiction: Its Nature, Faults and Virtues." In *The Science Fiction Novel: Imagination and Social Criticism*, 14-48. Chicago: Advent, 1971.

---. "Sky Lift." In *The Menace From Earth*, 115-28. New York: Signet, 1964.

---. "Happy Days Ahead" In *Expanded Universe: The New Worlds of Robert A. Heinlein*, 515-582. New York: Grosset & Dunlap, 1980.

Herbert, Frank. "Under Pressure (Part 1)." *Astounding Science Fiction*, November 1955, 6-66.

---. "Under Pressure (Part 2)." *Astounding Science Fiction*, December 1955, 79-126.

---. "Under Pressure (Part 3)." *Astounding Science Fiction*, January 1956, 80-135.

Jenkins, Will F. "Applied Science Fiction." *Analog Science Fiction / Science Fact*, November 1967, 108-24.

---. "A Logic Named Joe." *Astounding Science-Fiction*, March 1946, 139-54.

Johnston, Sean F. "Emmett Leith: Early work and influence." *Proceedings of 7th International Symposium on Display Holography* (2006): 2-7.

---. "Yuri Denisyuk: An Appreciation." *Proceedings of 7th International Symposium on Display Holography* (2006): 8-13.

Kraeuter, David W. "The U.S. Patents of Alexanderson, Carson, Colpitts, Davis, Gernsback, Hogan, Loomis, Pupin, Rider, Stone, and Stubblefield." *The AWA Review* 6 (1991): 155-84.

Leinster, Murray [Will F. Jenkins]. "Politics." *Amazing Stories*, June 1932, 268-79.

Leith, Emmett N. "Reflections on the origin and subsequent course of holography." *Proceedings of SPIE-IS&T Electronic Imaging* 5005 (2003): 431-38.

Luo, Zhongsheng, Jesse Manders and Jeff Yurek. "Television's Quantum-Dot Future." *IEEE Spectrum*, March 2018, 28-33, 52-53.

MacDonald, Anson [Robert A. Heinlein]. "Beyond This Horizon (Part 1)." *Astounding Science-Fiction*, April 1942, 9-50.

---. "Solution Unsatisfactory." *Astounding Science-Fiction*, May 1941, 56-86.

---. "Waldo." *Astounding Science-Fiction*, August 1942, 9-53.

McCann, Arthur [John W. Campbell, Jr.]. "Atomic Ringmaster." *Astounding Science-Fiction*. March 1940, 112-16.

---. "Isotope 235." *Astounding Science-Fiction*, August 1939, 70-71.

---. "Shhhhh – Don't Mention It!" *Astounding Science-Fiction*, August 1940, 104-14.

Newland, D. E. "Hawthorne, Sir William Rede (1913 – 2011)." *Oxford*

Dictionary of National Biography (January 2015). http://www.oxforddnb
.com/view/article/104135 (accessed April 10, 2016).

Parkinson, Bradford W., Stephen T. Powers et al. "Part 1: The Origins of GPS, and the Pioneers Who Launched the System." http://gpsworld.com/origins-gps-part-1/. (accessed December 25, 2017)

Ridley, R. T. "To be Taken with a Pinch of Salt: The Destruction of Carthage." *Classical Philology* 81, no. 2 (April 1986): 140-46.

Shelokhonov, Steve. "Ivan Yefremov, IMDb Mini Biography." https://www
.imdb.com/name/nm0947234/bio (accessed June 11, 2018).

Smith. E. E. "Gray Lensman (Part 4)" *Astounding Science-Fiction*, January 1940, 102-53.

Strauss, Mark. "Ten Inventions Inspired by Science Fiction." https://www.smithsonianmag.com/science-nature/ten-inventions-inspired-by-science-fiction-128080674/ (accessed December 23, 2017).

Swanwick, Michael. "Growing Up in the Future." https://www.michael swanwick.com/ nonfic/future.html (accessed July 15, 2006).

"The Late William Hooper." *The Telegraphic Journal and Electrical Review* 6, no. 137 (October 15, 1878): 416-17.

Weber, Bruce. "Jack Cover, 88, Physicist Who Invented the Taser Stun Gun, Dies." https://www.nytimes.com/2009/02/16/us/16cover.html (accessed March 10, 2018).

Yefremov, Ivan. "From the author." (In Russian) http://www.noogen.su /iefremov/ stories.htm (accessed November 10, 2017).

Books

Alvarez, Luis W. *Alvarez: Adventures of a Physicist*. Lexington MA: Plunkett Lake Press, 2017. Ebook.

Ashley, Mike and Robert A. W. Lowndes. *The Gernsback Days: A study of the evolution of modern science fiction from 1911 to 1936*. Holicong PA: Wildside Press, 2004.

Bailey, J. O. *Pilgrims Through Space and Time: Trends and Patterns in Scientific and Utopian Fiction*. New York: Argus Books, 1947.

Berger. Albert I. *The Magic that Works: John W. Campbell and the American*

Response to Technology. San Bernardino: The Borgo Press, 1993.

Boslaugh, David L. *When Computers Went to Sea: The Digitization of the United States Navy.* Los Alamitos, CA: IEEE Computer Society, 1999.

Brake, Mark L. and Neil Hook. *Different Engines: How science drives fiction and fiction drives science.* London: Macmillan, 2008.

Chisholm, Donald. *Waiting for Dead Men's Shoes: Origins and Development of the U.S. Navy's Officer Personnel System, 1793-1941.* Stanford: Stanford University Press, 2001.

CIC Handbook for Destroyers, Pacific Fleet. 1943.

Clarke, Arthur C. *Profiles of the Future.* New York: Holt, Rinehart and Winston, 1984.

Compton, Arthur Holly. *Atomic Quest: A Personal Narrative.* New York: Oxford University Press, 1956.

Cromie, Robert. *The Crack of Doom.* London: Digby, Long & Co., 1895. Ebook.

Forward, Robert L. *Indistinguishable From Magic.* New York: Baen, 1995.

Franklin, H. Bruce. *War Stars: The Superweapon and the American Imagination.* New York: Oxford University Press, 1988.

Friedman, Norman. *Naval Firepower: Battleship Guns and Gunnery in the Dreadnought Era.* Annapolis: Naval Institute Press, 2008.

Gebhard, Louis A. *Evolution of Naval Radio-Electronics and Contributions of the Naval Research Laboratory.* Washington: Naval Research Laboratory, 1979.

Gertner, Jon. *The Idea Factory: Bell Labs and the Great Age of American Innovation.* New York: Penguin Press, 2012.

Gifford, James. *Robert A. Heinlein: A Reader's Companion.* Sacramento: Nitrosyncretic Press, 2000.

Heilbron, J. L. and Robert W. Seidel. *Lawrence and his Laboratory: A History of the Lawrence Berkeley Laboratory, Volume I.* Berkeley: University of California Press, 1989.

Heinlein, Robert A. *Double Star,* New York: Signet, n.d.

---. *Stranger in a Strange Land.* New York: Avon, 1966.

Herbert, Brian. *Dreamer of Dune: The Biography of Frank Herbert.* New York: Tom Doherty Associates, 2003.

Hewlett, Richard G. and Oscar E. Anderson, Jr. *The New World 1939/1946, A History of The United States Atomic Energy Commission, Volume I.* University Park PA: The Pennsylvania State University Press, 1962.

Hiltzik, Michael. *Big Science: Ernest Lawrence and the Invention That Launched the Military-Industrial Complex.* New York: Simon & Schuster, 2015.

Howeth, Linwood S. *History of Communications in the United States Navy.* Washington: GPO, 1963.

Lake, Simon and Herbert Corey. *Submarine: The Autobiography of Simon Lake.* New York: D. Appleton-Century, 1938.

Lanouette, William with Bela Silard. *Genius in The Shadows: A Biography of Leo Szilard, The Man Behind the Bomb.* Chicago: The University of Chicago Press, 1994.

Lloyd, Peter. *Combustion in the Gas Turbine: A Survey of War-time Research and Development.* London: Her Majesty's Stationery Office, 1952.

McCarthy, Wil. *Hacking Matter.* Multimedia Edition, 2003.

O'Reilly, Timothy. *Frank Herbert.* New York: Frederick Ungar Publishing, 1981.

Patterson, William H., Jr. *Robert A. Heinlein: In Dialogue with His Century: Volume 1, 1907-1948: Learning Curve.* New York: Tom Doherty Associates, 2010.

---. *Robert A. Heinlein: In Dialogue with His Century: Volume 2, 1948-1988: The Man Who Learned Better.* New York: Tom Doherty Associates, 2014.

Pierre, Jean-Marc. "The 1956 Suez Crisis and The United Nations." Master's Thesis, US Army Command and General Staff College, 2004.

Preston, S. Tolver. *Physics of the Ether.* London: E & F. N. Spon, 1875.

Qualcomm Tricorder XPrize Competition Guidelines, 14 November 2016, Version 31. https://tricorder.xprize.org/sites/default/files/qtxp_guidelines _v31_11_14_2016.pdf.

Pavelec, Sterling M. *The Jet Race and the Second World War.* Annapolis: Naval Institute Press, 2007.

Resnick, Mike and Joe Siclari (Eds.). *Worldcon Guest of Honor Speeches.* Deerfield IL: ISFiC Press, 2006.

Rhodes, Richard. *The Making of the Atomic Bomb.* New York: Simon and Schuster, 1986.

Sherborne, Michael. *H. G. Wells: Another Kind of Life*. London: Peter Owen Publishers, 2013. Ebook.

Smith, David C. *H. G. Wells: Desperately Mortal*. New Haven: Yale University Press, 1986.

Soddy, Frederick. *The Interpretation of Radium*. New York: G. P. Putnam's Sons, 1909.

Stallings, Billee J. and Jo-An J. Evans. *Murray Leinster: The Life and Works*. Jefferson NC: McFarland, 2011.

Stafeev, S. K. (Ed.) *The Way to Invention* (In Russian). St. Petersburg: ITMO University, 2015. http://www.hih.org.gr/web/viewer.html?file=/images/attachments/Book_About_ Yuri_Denisyuk_ITMO_2015.pdf

Stimson, George W. *Introduction to Airborne Radar, 2nd edition*. Raleigh: SciTech, 1998.

Wadle, Ryan D. "United States Navy Fleet Problems and the Development of Carrier Aviation, 1929-1933." Master's Thesis, Texas A&M, 2005.

Weart, Spencer R. and Gertrud Weiss Szilard (Eds.). *Leo Szilard: His Version of the Facts*. Cambridge: The MIT Press, 1980.

Webster, T. and Mrs. Parkes. *An Encyclopædia of Domestic Economy*. New York: Harper & Brothers, 1855.

Wells, H. G. *The World Set Free: A Story of Mankind*. London: Macmillan, 1914.

Wolters, Timothy S. *Information at Sea: Shipboard Command and Control in the U.S. Navy, from Mobile Bay to Okinawa*. Baltimore: Johns Hopkins University Press, 2013.

---. "Managing a Sea of Information: Shipboard Command and Control in the United States Navy, 1899-1945." Ph.D. diss., MIT, 2003.

Wysocki, Edward M. Jr. *An ASTOUNDING War: Science Fiction and World War II*. North Charleston: CreateSpace, 2015.

---. *The Great Heinlein Mystery: Science Fiction, Innovation and Naval Technology*. North Charleston: CreateSpace, 2012.

Yefremov, I. *Stories*. Moscow: Foreign Language Publishing House, 1954.

ACKNOWLEDGEMENTS

I will begin by thanking Charles Hall for providing me with information on the development of the waterbed. As I commented in Chapter 7, every article on the subject of Mr. Hall begins with him in 1968 as a graduate student who has just invented the waterbed. He kindly consented to answer my questions that covered his early life, how he wound up at San Francisco State College and how his design project led to the waterbed. I am also grateful to Darlene Tong, who is a Subject Librarian at the J. Paul Leonard Library at SFSU. She was able to provide answers to my questions about the School of Design and Hall's project. She also passed my questions to some members of the faculty of the School of Design. I would like to collectively thank them for their responses.

The largest problem that I encountered was in my research on Yuri Denisyuk. Any source that I was able to locate in English only mentioned when and where he was born, that he was in Leningrad during the Siege and then what he did to develop his form of holography. There were many details of his life that could not be found anywhere. I did eventually discover a book, *The Way to Invention*, that contains much information on the life of Denisyuk. There was just one small problem; the book was in Russian. I had taken two years of Russian as a college undergraduate more years ago than I am willing to admit. I was able to pick out the sections of the book that contained what I needed, but I did not feel capable of coming up with a reliable translation. I made some enquiries and was able to find someone to assist me. Luke Jeske and I went over those sections together and he was able to provide just the information I needed. While I am grateful for Mr. Jeske's skill in translation and his comments on what I wrote based on the translation, I assume full responsibility for the accuracy of the material and how it has been presented to the reader.

In my research into Sir William Hawthorne and the Dracone, I was able to obtain much useful material from the Churchill Archives Centre at Churchill College, Cambridge University. I would like to thank Heidi Egginton for her assistance in locating the material I needed. The material obtained from the Churchill Archives Centre is used by permission of the estate of Sir William Hawthorne.

The material from the Smith-Campbell letter is used by permission of AC Projects, Inc., 7376 Walker Road, Fairview TN, 37062.

All material related to Robert Heinlein is reproduced by permission of the Robert A. & Virginia Heinlein Prize Trust.

My thanks to Bill Higgins for providing me with a copy of the Steiner interview of Robert Cornog.

My thanks to Dr. Charbel Rizk for his technical comments regarding the infrared rangefinder in "Politics."

My thanks to Janice Goldblum at the National Academy of Sciences Archives for locating and providing me with the Minutes and Reports of the Advisory Committee of the National Academy on Uranium Disintegration.

My thanks to Caleb Laning's daughter, Lillian Giornelli, for permission to quote from her father's letters, papers and records.

My thanks to Penny Publications LLC/Dell Magazines for permission to use the cover image of the November 1939 issue of *Astounding Science-Fiction*.

Finally, I would like to thank Jeff Mitchell and Gary Roen for the valuable feedback that they provided to me while this book was being put together.

INDEX

G

Gabor, Dennis, 27, 39-44, 48, 50-51, 52, 54
Gernsback, Hugo, 93, 119, 133-35
Gherardi, Bancroft, 90
Goddard, Robert H., 7-8
Gow, A. S. F., 67
GPS, 8-9
Gray Lensman, 120-22, 129-30, 154

H

Hall, Charles, 101-06, 108, 109-11
"The Happy Days Ahead", 106-07
Hawthorne, Sir William, 56-57, 58-60, 65-70, 71-73
Heinlein, Robert A., 1-3, 6, 7, 13-14, 79-80, 84-86, 87-89, 91, 93-100, 103, 106-07, 110
Heinlein, Leslyn, 88, 96, 97
Helium, 21-22, 29-30, 75, 76, 80-82.
Herbert
    Brian, 70-71
    Frank, 60-65, 71
Holography, 35, 39, 42, 43-44, 47, 48-51, 52-54
Hooper, William, 100-01
Hottel, Hoyt, 56, 60
How William Shatner Changed the World, 11
Hydraulic bed (see Waterbed)
Hydrogen 29, 33-34, 75, 80-82

I

Identification Friend or Foe, 124, 130
IFF (see Identification Friend or Foe)
Infrared, 147
Inspiration, 7, 8
The Interpretation of Radium, 22-23, 24, 29
Isotopes, 21, 30, 33-34, 75, 80, 84, 85, 91
"Isotope 235", 84

J

Jenkins, Will, 137-44, 147-49, 155

K

Kästner, Erich, 10

ABOUT THE AUTHOR

Edward M. Wysocki, Jr. received his Ph.D. in Electrical Engineering from Johns Hopkins University. This was followed by over three decades with a major defense contractor. Dr. Wysocki is a member of The Heinlein Society and the Science Fiction Research Association. This is his third book-length effort in the field of science fiction. The first was *The Great Heinlein Mystery*, which explored a claim by Robert Heinlein that one of his stories influenced World War II naval technology. The second was *An ASTOUNDING War*, which looked at the connections between science fiction and World War II. All of the books of Dr. Wysocki reflect his interests in history, technology and science fiction.

Made in United States
Orlando, FL
13 January 2024

42436830R00108